THE SACRED AND THE SUBVERSIVE: POLITICAL WITCH-HUNTS AS NATIONAL RITUALS

by
ALBERT BERGESEN

Department of Sociology
University of Arizona

SOCIETY FOR THE SCIENTIFIC STUDY OF RELIGION
MONOGRAPH SERIES, STORRS, CONNECTICUT
ISBN 0-932566-03-0

Library of Congress Catalogue Card Number: 84-061370
International Standard Book Number: -0932566-03-0

Editor's Introduction

Sociologists grapple with no more important question than how social units ensure some degree of conformity to group shared expectations of behavior. Emile Durkheim suggested the importance of public ritual in social control. Following Guy E. Swanson and Kai Erikson in their investigation and development of this Durkheimian idea, Albert Bergesen, in *The Sacred and the Subversive: Political Witch-Hunts as National Rituals*, seeks to understand the creation of subversion as a ritual mechanism that renews sacred national values.

The SSSR Monograph Series intends to represent the wide range—both methodologically and substantively—of the field of the scientific study of religion. There is a particular hope that the present volume will stimulate further attempts to explore the many relevant variables whose measurement is especially elusive in cross-national studies.

James R. Wood
Editor

TABLE OF CONTENTS

LIST OF TABLES

LIST OF FIGURES

INTRODUCTION

The Durkheimian study of religion usually involves looking at society's myths and symbols, its collective representations in his terms, and the rites and rituals which are performed to these totemic images. Often this research takes the form of qualitative descriptions of symbols, rites, and primitive religions, the ethnographies of anthropologists and comparative religionists. In good part this approach is dictated by the very elusive nature of the subject matter; ideas of gods, spirits, or totemic forces are, to put it mildly, difficult to quantify and study with statistical techniques.

There have been, though, studies in the Durkheimian tradition which have utilized the techniques of quantitative social science. In particular I am thinking of Guy E. Swanson's *The Birth of the Gods* (1964) and Kai T. Erikson's *The Wayward Puritans* (1966). Both Swanson and Erikson took central ideas from Durkheim's larger understanding of the role of ritual in the reproduction of social reality and subjected them to empirical test. Swanson looked at the relationship between the corporate organization of society, what he took to be Durkheim's notion of society "sui generis," and the collective representations of that corporateness, society's gods and spirits. Swanson's proposition was simple: vary the corporate organization of the society and you will vary the nature of the symbolizations of that corporateness, namely the group's experiences with all powerful gods and spirits. Erikson looked more at the role of ritual in the reaffirmation of group life, paying particular attention to how a community responds to a crisis in collective existence, what he called a "boundary crisis." He argued that a community will commense to ritually persecute imaginary enemies—conduct a witch-hunt—to manufacture moral deviants as a means of ritually reaffirming the group's problematical values and collective purposes.

Swanson's work derives more directly from Durkheim's *Elementary Forms* (1965), while Erikson follows the lead in the *Division of Labor* (1933) where Durkheim speaks of the solidarity that is produced by punishing crime and moral deviance. It would seem on the surface that questions of religion and crime are quite different, yet a closer examination of their social foundations reveals a profound similarity, for both are elements in the overall process of renewing and reaffirming collective sentiments and thereby reproducing group life itself. Not only do the gods need their worshipers, but moral sentiments also need their deviant and criminal opposite.

In this monograph these two lines of thinking are brought together to explain one of the most interesting aspects of modern civil religion (Bellah, 1967; Goodin, 1981), the political witch-hunt. If we can consider the sacred political ideologies of the modern political community as a Durkheimian collective representation, then their symbolic opposite, the creation of subversion through the political witch-hunt, can be seen as one of the key ritual mechanisms for the periodic renewal of sacred national values.

Following the theoretical lead of Durkheim and the quantitative research of Swanson and Erikson, this monograph proposes a general theoretical model designed to explain why some nations experience higher rates of witch-hunting than others. To test this model data on witch-hunting activity is gathered by coding political events from the *New York Times* for a sample of 26 nations between 1950 and 1955.

ACKNOWLEDGMENT

I would like to thank the Laboratory for Social Research of Stanford University for a small grant which facilitated much of this research. The coding process was long and boring, and the level of commitment and standards maintained by Joanie Woolf, Jane Wagner, and Ken Woods was phenomenal, undoubtedly making this a much better study. My dissertation committee, John W. Meyer, Morris Zelditch Jr., and W. Richard Scott provided helpful comments on earlier drafts and encouragement throughout the project. I especially would like to thank Richard Rubinson, Chris Chase-Dunn, and John W. Meyer who, from the inception of this project through its completion, offered intellectual support, often needed criticism, and indispensable methodological advice in translating what began as a vague Durkheimian idea about "the people" as a collective representation, into a researchable problem. Their presence has left an indelible mark on this piece of research.

Finally, Robert Wuthnow and James Wood provided helpful comments on preparing this manuscript for the SSSR monograph series.

CHAPTER 1

THEORIES OF POLITICAL WITCH-HUNTS

The literature on political witch-hunts is immense and primarily centered upon analysis and descriptions of particular historical events. There are studies of the Stalinist purges (Conquest, 1968; Connor, 1972; Gouldner, 1978; Brzezinski, 1956), the Chinese Cultural Revolution (Solomon, 1971; Bridgham, 1967; Hinton, 1972), or similar Chinese rectification campaigns (MacFarquhar, 1960; Goldman, 1967; Baum and Teiwes, 1968), and the McCarthy anti-Communist hysteria which swept the United States in the early fifties (Bell, 1964; Lipset, 1955; Parsons, 1955; Caute, 1978; Navasky, 1980).

Discussions of political witch-hunts in more general terms are few, focusing upon explanations of the functions of political purges and terror in the maintenance of one-party regimes, and interpretations of McCarthyism as an instance of status politics.

Political Purges and Totalitarian States

In an attempt to understand the unique features of polities such as Nazi Germany and a Stalinist Soviet Union, a literature dealing with "totalitarian" societies has emerged (Friedrich and Brzezinski, 1956; Arendt, 1973).

From this perspective political purges, as a type of witch-hunt, are viewed as an integral institutional feature of totalitarian societies. The purge, in effect, is required by a political system intent upon "total" social control of its members. More specifically this literature suggests three functions of purges in totalitarian systems.

Maintaining Political Elites. Brzezinski (1956) argues that purges and political terror are "instruments of the state" that can be mobilized by elites to eliminate both real and imagined political opposition. The disruption of the party ranks and government bureaucracy through periodic purges acts to prevent the crystallization of interests which might form against the regime. Similarly the extension of the purge and political terror into ever widening circles of the more general population is thought to further atomize the citizenry and prevent the emergence of social alliances which could form potential opposition.

This notion that the purge constitutes a means for the elimination of enemies is not in accord with the historical record as to when these purges seem to occur. That is, the most violent and dramatic purges, as in the case of the Soviet Union, occurred after the opposition to the Stalinist forces had been all but eliminated. The same thing can be said about China where, prior to the Cultural Revolution, party dominance operated not only in the political system but also in virtually every area of organized social life.[1]

What is even more interesting is the fact that there seems to be an inverse relationship between the presence of enemies of the regime and the outbreaks of large scale purges. As Arendt noted:

What happened instead was that terror increased both in Soviet Russia and Nazi Germany in inverse ratio to the existence of internal political opposition, so that it

---

[1]See Tang Tsou (1969) for a discussion of the Party dominance of Chinese institutions just prior to the Cultural Revolution.

looked as though political opposition had not been the pretext of terror . . . but the last impediment to its full fury.[2]

Further, these types of political systems also seem quite immune to the presence of internal coups. Again Arendt (1973:418) notes "the complete absence of successful or unsuccessful palace revolutions is one of the most remarkable characteristics of totalitarian dictatorships."

Release of Structurally Induced Strain. The various bureaucrats and party cadre charged with political crimes form, in effect, objects upon which these societies can cathect those frustrations, anxieties and aggressive impulses that are generated within a tightly run totalitarian state. In this fashion, argue Inkeles (1950) and Brzezinski (1956), the regime leadership can direct attention from itself and its failure upon newly created scapegoats.

Elimination of Bureaucratic Stagnation. Totalitarian regimes, because of their ideological commitment to socially transform the society they inherit, purportedly face the problem of maintaining a high degree of morale and commitment amongst the cadre who are entrusted with carrying out the revolutionary program. The construction of an elaborate bureaucratic social structure authorized to implement any number of ideological goals creates a series of organizations and social positions, the occupancy of which may become an end in itself. The bureaucrat comes to serve either himself or the needs of his bureaucratic establishment at the expense of larger political goals. The purging of party cadre, military personnel, and the government bureaucracy functions to remove those cadre who are no longer serving larger political goals. The bureaucratic ranks are thereby periodically replenished with cadre possessing the necessary political commitment.

Although bureaucratic personnel periodically require replacement it seems doubtful that the ritual degradation, collective hysteria, and public proclamations that accompany large scale purges and trials are that necessary for periodic personnel changes. The point here is similar to the "elimination of potential enemies" argument: namely, if the mere removal of individuals or even groups is all that is at stake then the accompanying elaborate charges, public confessions, and self-admissions of deviation that inevitably accompany these purges seem unnecessary.

McCarthyism and Status Politics

The idea of status politics, which has been employed to explain various American protest and reform movements such as the Progressive Movement (Hofstader, 1955), the Temperance Movement, Prohibition (Gusfield, 1963), and the radical right (Bell, 1964; Lipset, 1955), has also been applied to the McCarthy period (Bell, 1960). The basic idea is that these assorted movements represent a response to the transformation of America from a basically rural, agrarian and politically decentralized nation to an urban, industrial and politically centralized state. This social transformation created strains for various status groups which found their status position, as opposed to their economic or class position, being undermined and replaced by new groups and new standards. These status groups share little in common except their common predicament of being, in Bell's words, "dispossessed." They include the traditional military establishment, which finds its authority undermined by the increasing use of technicians and so-called

---

[2]Arendt (1973:393)

defense department intellectuals, the small businessman who resents increased government controls and attention given large corporations, and the small town Protestant American who finds his central values giving way to the ascendancy of urban life and metropolitan culture.

The application of this line of explanation to McCarthyism has been made by Bell (1960) who argues that the anti-communism theme of these movements represents symbolic "targets on whom they can vent their dispossession." The feared communists and their suspected location in the State Department or in elite universities such as Harvard, symbolize for these groups the larger social transformation to an urban cosmopolitan society.

These ideas of status protest and status politics, though, are designed to explain the actions of particular groups within the larger society, and do not lend themselves to answering the question of why some societies experience higher rates of political deviance than others. My unit of analysis is not particular groups within the society (e.g., groups experiencing status stress) but whole national societies.

Adequacy of Present Theories

This Monograph is concerned with a comparative analysis of political witch-hunts and with predicting why some societies experience higher rates of distinctly political deviance than others. The ideas generated by students of totalitarian societies and status politics as general explanations for the appearance of political deviance seem inadequate for the following reasons.

Lack of Generality. First, neither perspective is general enough to explain rates of political deviance across a sample of national societies. The totalitarian explanation is limited to highly mobilized states, where most aspects of institutional life are strictly controlled from the political center. Political witch-hunts, such as the McCarthy period, have also appeared in non-totalitarian societies, and there seems to be a great deal of variation in the amount and kind of political witch-hunting activity in which national societies engage. At one end of the continuum are societies such as the Soviet Union or the People's Republic of China, which have experienced numerous episodes of searching public institutions for those who are undermining revolutionary goals, and at the other end are countries such as Sweden and Norway which have had very little experience with the purported presence of "enemies of the Republic." Finally, somewhere in between there are countries such as the United States or Great Britain which have only occasionally found disloyal elements in their midst.

Political witch-hunts are found in a great variety of national societies, only some bearing the social characteristics known as totalitarian.[3] A very similar problem exists with the status politics explanation where the units of analysis are specific status groups experiencing a variety of strains and stresses and not national societies.

Although ideas about totalitarian societies and status politics are more general than the case studies of particular political witch-hunts, they are not sufficiently general to permit an analysis of political deviance across all national societies. Even taking these theoretical positions on their own grounds, they are still inadequate when it comes to

---

[3]Arendt further limits her definition of totalitarianism to only certain periods, "up to now we know only two authentic historical forms of totalitarian domination: the dictatorship of national socialism after 1938, and the dictatorship of Bolshevism since 1930." (1973:419)

explaining some of the most unique and sociologically distinctive aspects of purges, rectification campaigns, or Senate investigations. Political witch-hunts possess two distinguishing characteristics that are explained in only the most cursory fashion by the perspectives under review.

Ritualistic Handling of Political Subversives. Political purges inevitably involve public ceremonies of the most ritualistic character. Show trials, extensive press coverage, and public confessions are the now familiar hallmarks of the modern political purge. The elimination of political opposition or the replacement of bureaucratic personnel could seemingly be managed without the accompanying public spectacles. Similarly, the notion that the ritual of purges forms part of the regimes arsenal of "terror" required to maintain control over the populace, fails to recognize the legitimacy and stability enjoyed by one-party states.

The seeming ritualistic encounters between the defenders of the nation and all that it represents, and those alien and subversive elements intent upon destroying the very foundation of national existence, must be explained as more than a mere excuse for political elites to eliminate their enemies; particularly when the most dramatic encounters seem to occur after all internal political opposition has been vanquished.

What Constitutes Crimes Against the State? Another unique feature of political witch-hunts is the great variation in what can be defined as a crime against the country, nation, or people. More than mere variation in the types of crime, the striking feature of witch-hunts is the trivial and non-political character of many of the supposed counter-revolutionary or subversive acts. This feature of all political witch-hunts, that almost any activity can be considered a crime against the state, is captured by Talmon in his description of the reign of terror during the French Revolution.

> To have remained silent on some past and half-forgotten occasion, where one would have spoken; to have spoken where it was better to hold one's peace; to have shown apathy where eagerness was called for, and enthusiasm where diffidence was necessary; to have consorted with somebody whom a patriot should have shunned; avoided one now deserved to be befriended; not to have shown a virtuous disposition, or not to have led a life of virtue—such and other "sins" came to be accounted as capital offenses, classifying the sinners as members of that immense chain of treason comprising the foreign plot, Royalism, federalism, bureaucratic sabotage, food speculation, immoral wealth, and viscious self perversion.[4]

Political witch-hunts whether the foreign plot during the French Revolution, the McCarthy anti-communism crusade, or the Chinese Cultural Revolution, have as one of their most distinguishing properties the fact that almost any activity can become a political crime. Similarly, individuals far removed from centers of political power, and with neither the seeming motivation nor the organizational base to engage in overthrowing the regime can find themselves accused of subversive activities. This is a feature of all witch-hunts dismissed by theorists of totalitarian societies as a purge getting out of control and devouring innocent people, and by students of status politics as the paranoid projections of groups experiencing some form of status stress.

---

[4]Talmon (1970:129)

4

Summary and Conclusion

Political witch-hunts are accompanied by trials, confessions, investigations, and propaganda campaigns that seem way out of proportion with either a response to the presence of actual spies and treasonous cliques or as a means of eliminating political opposition. Similarly it seems that almost any member of the society can be found to be participating in one form of subversive activity or another. Charges of subversive activity are also not limited to those political circles who are either in a position to take state power, such as military or political elites, or dissident groups who could conceivably mobilize opposition to the regime. Groups far from the centers of political power— teachers, artists, writers, and agricultural workers have been accused of "taking the capitalist road" in socialist states or having "communist tendencies" in capitalist states. The substance of plays, the content of art, and the nature of social acquaintances have all been considered at one time or another as "counter-revolutionary," "treasonous," or "un-American." That the rank and file populace and the most trivial of activities can be considered as seditious and treasonous is a social fact not to be dismissed as incidental to the real purposes and functions of witch-hunts. They are a significant aspect in the very definition of political witch-hunts and as such require a substantive sociological explanation.

CHAPTER 2
A THEORY OF POLITICAL DEVIANCE

In Chapter 1 theories of the origins and functions of political witch-hunts were found inadequate in that they could not (1) provide a generalized theoretical scheme capable of explaining the appearance of witch-hunts across a sample of national societies, or (2) of generating a sociologically satisfying account as to why these events are accompanied by such extensive ritual; why trivial acts can become crimes against the nation; or why individuals with no seeming intention of taking political action against the state can come to be considered as subversive or treasonous. This chapter puts forth a theoretical scheme to explain these properties of witch-hunts.

Crimes Against the Nation: Corporate Crime

Political crime can mean many things. It can refer to the study of collective violence and civil disorders,[5] or it can refer to the social processes whereby individual acts of vandalism, assassination, terrorist bombing, or other "normal crimes," come to be defined by political authorities as constituting distinctly political acts.[6] In short, political crime could refer to any number of different processes. But, for this research the term will be used in a very specific manner.

Since the term *political crime* has numerous well understood meanings, the notion of *corporate crime* will be introduced. *Corporate crime refers to those activities which are defined by legitimate political authorities to be acts committed against the interests and purposes of the corporate nation-state.* For example, during the French Revolution there suddenly appeared counter-revolutionaries, loyalist agents, foreign spies, and clandestine clergy, who the Jacobins saw as a threat to all that the revolution had fought to achieve.[7] What all these groups shared in common was their purported intent to undermine the newly established revolutionary society. Similarly, during the Stalinist trials of the late nineteen thirties, there appeared Wreckers, Trotskyites, and enemies of the Soviet people; during the McCarthy period there were Communists, Communist sympathizers, spies, and other seditious elements, and finally, during the Chinese Cultural Revolution of the late 1960s there were capitalist roaders, revisionists, rightists, and ultra-leftists. In all these societies there appeared groups who possessed the common characteristic of being understood to be somehow acting against or undermining the very essence of the corporate nation itself.

Emile Durkheim: Crime and Moral Solidarity

One of the most provocative sociological approaches to the study of crime has been that of Emile Durkheim.[8] One of Durkheim's primary concerns was over the question of

---

[5]See the readings in the collections of Fierabend and Gurr (1972), Graham and Gurr (1969), Gillespie and Nesvold (1971).
[6]See Turner (1969) or Silver (1969).
[7]For a discussion of crimes during the Reign of Terror see Greer (1935) or Palmer (1941).

what made some activities criminal and others not. It became obvious that the presence of community punishment was not a function of the danger that particular activities posed to the functioning of the community itself. Many white collar crimes which could clearly upset the economic functioning of the society were less severely punished than crimes of petty theft. The community reacts to certain actions not because they, in Durkheim's famous phrasing, are criminal, for they become "criminal" because the community reacts to them. Activities are criminal because they violate communities' mores or "shock the common conscience." No action is inherently criminal; all that is required is the violation of some community norm. Punishment, therefore, acts not to reform the offender but to bring the community together to ritually reaffirm that aspect of the normative order which was violated. As Durkheim noted:

> Crime brings together upright consciences and concentrates them. We have only to notice what happens, particularly in a small town, when some moral scandal has just been committed. They stop each other on the street, they visit each other, they seek to come together to talk of the event and to wax indignant in common.[9]

Durkheim further reasoned that far from being disfunctional for a society, the presence of crime was, in fact, quite functional. The periodic punctuation of social life with normative violations functioned to bring the community together in common moral indignation and thereby ritually reaffirm the common moral order.

Kai T. Erikson: The Community Creation of Deviance

Erikson (1966) took the basic Durkheimian assumption about the functional quality of crime and added another important assumption. Erikson reasoned that if the presence of deviance was functional, why should society wait for some periodic violation of community mores? The society, in effect, need not wait for individuals to stray across its moral boundaries to attain the consequent positive result of intensifying moral solidarity if it could create the deviance itself. This assumption has taken the original Durkheimian position as to the functions of and naturalness of deviance, and added another important assumption as to the origins of crime.

Deviance can, therefore, come about in two ways: (1) individuals can cross the moral boundaries, the original Durkheim position, or (2) the boundaries themselves can be shifted by the community and thereby reclassify groups and individuals as deviants, the Erikson assumption. For instance, consider a university professor who has been teaching courses on Russian social institutions for the past twenty or thirty years. During this time his activity did not violate normative boundaries and was not considered to be "un-American" or subversive in character. There then appears the McCarthy period and suddenly he finds his work being defined as disloyal and un-American. The content of his classes have not changed. He has not, by his activity, crossed or violated some stationary moral boundary. What has changed is the definition of what constitutes subversive activity and this shifting boundary has now moved over to include his course on Russian institutions.

Every social community possesses a set of institutional arrangements allocated the responsibility of defining moral boundaries, and hence, deviance. The police, courts,

---

[8] Particularly the chapter on Mechanical Solidarity (pp. 70-110) in Durkheim's *Division of Labor*.
[9] Durkheim (1933:102)

jails, prisons, and mental hospitals are modern institutional arrangements which function to define deviant behavior and thereby to establish or reestablish the ever shifting symbolic boundary separating the deviant from the normal, thereby allowing the community to create and maintain a certain volume of deviance. The reaffirmation of moral solidarity need not wait for members of the society to commit "crimes themselves," that is, for the individuals to violate some rule. The community can, on its own, create deviance by processing groups and individuals through its institutions of social control, thereby publicly reaffirming the character and definition of its own moral order.

Erikson further reasoned that since deviance functions to maintain the moral boundaries of a community, when there appeared a dramatic increase in the volume of deviance it must be a consequence of some crisis in these moral boundaries. The community, through its institutions of social control, responds to this crisis by creating deviance. The definition of individuals as beyond the community's moral order functions to redraw or reestablish the threatened boundary. For instance, in his example of the Massachusetts Bay Colony, the withdrawal of the Colony's Charter by Charles II created a crisis in the meaning of collective existence for the Bay community, and the subsequent appearance of witches in Salem helped to reestablish the moral character of the Colony.

Erikson's boundary crisis theory, though, does not explain the particular features of political deviance that are of interest in this research.

Cross-national Rates of Witch-Hunting

The boundary crisis hypothesis explains the appearance of deviance within only one society and has no theoretical implications for why some societies should experience more deviance than others. Erikson's concern was with differing rates within a society; that is, why the rate or volume of deviance should dramatically increase, creating what he termed a "crime wave." If we assume that the rates of political deviance vary across a sample of societies, and we are to use Erikson's boundary crisis hypothesis, must we also assume a similar variation in the rates of boundary crises? Or, are there different kinds of crises, such that some generate a larger volume of deviance than others? Or is there a range of boundary crises that a society can experience, such that those societies which have a larger volume of deviance are perhaps experiencing different kinds of crises than those societies which have a small volume of political deviance? Finally, are there characteristics of some societies which enable them to withstand a crisis and therefore not require the presence of deviance? All of these exist as theoretical possibilities within the present formulation of Erikson's theory, but there is no way of knowing which might be the case.

Further, when it appears that political crime is endemic in some societies, must we also assert constant boundary crises for these nations? China, for instance, has been constantly preoccupied with routing out counter-revolutionaries, reactionaries, capitalist roaders, rightists and ultra-leftists, but it seems highly implausible that for every new rectification campaign or other witch-hunting activity that there has to be a simultaneous crisis in moral boundaries. A boundary crisis seems a more plausible explanation for an occasional outbreak of deviance, such as the Salem witch trials, or the Cultural Revolution. The interest here, though, is with comparative rates of deviance. That is, with comparing whole national societies and being able to theoretically predict which ones should have the higher rates of political deviance. For the appearance of any particular witch-hunt, or any particular increase in the volume of deviance, the Erikson notion of a boundary crisis is a much more plausible theoretical position.

The Distribution of Deviance Throughout the Social Structure

Erikson's formulation asserts that a large volume of deviance will appear; its distribution within a society's social structure is left unspecified. Political subversives are usually not discovered at large; they are embedded within certain institutional areas, like the government bureaucracy, educational institutions, or military facilities. Further, different nations seem to find different institutions infected with deviance. Some, such as the United States during the McCarthy period, discovered deviance primarily within political institutions such as the State Department. While others, like China during the Cultural Revolution, found "those taking the capitalist road" in virtually all aspects of social life. Whereas in the United States deviance was discovered principally within one institutional area, in China the discovery of subversive elements occurred in the army, the party bureaucracy, the government bureaucracy, on agricultural communes and within educational institutions.

A general formulation of political deviance should be capable of predicting the relative distribution of deviance throughout a nation's social structure. That is, in which societies should we expect deviance to be more extensively distributed throughout their institutional space, and in which societies should the discovery of deviance be limited to a few institutional areas? This is an important empirical aspect of political deviance for which there is no present explanation within the boundary crisis formulation.

Like Erikson, I assume that political deviance is not an inherent quality of either individuals or their actions, but a label conferred by the larger society. The authorized agents of the community, through the use of trials, accusations, investigations, purges and rectification campaigns, create subversive individuals by labeling them as such. I similarly assume along with Durkheim and Erikson that the function of creating political deviance is related to questions of social solidarity. But, I differ from Erikson by not attributing the appearance of witch-hunts to some kind of social crisis. *Instead of arguing that deviance acts to reestablish unstable moral bounds, I assert that political deviance dramatizes that which is permanent and enduring in group relations—the corporate nature of modern societies.*

The theory that will be developed here is based on two sets of ideas derived from Durkheim's *Elementary Forms of the Religious Life*: (a) that social rites performed to representations of the social collectivity act to periodically redefine the meaning of these symbolizations, and (b) that these representations can be infused into or immanent within the things and structure of everyday life.

The Ritual Function of Deviance in Creating and Maintaining Collective Representations

Two lines of thinking have derived from Durkheim's analysis of religious ritual and religious myth and his analysis of the social functions of crime. Interestingly enough, although his work in religion and his work in crime both have a common concern with the function of ritual activity in creating and maintaining cultural material, whether collective representations as in the analysis of primitive religion or moral boundaries in the analysis of crime, there has been little contact between later students of Durkheim's sociology of religion and Durkheim's sociology of deviance.

Erikson's analysis of the community creation of crime clearly implies that the action taken by various institutions of social control, whether police, courts, the legal system, prisons, etc., is of a ritualistic character. That is, the concern is not with apprehending those individuals because of the danger they pose to the community, but rather, with apprehending them so that the particular moral boundary in question can be symbolically reaffirmed, making the action of social control institutions ritualistic in character.

What is interesting then, is to compare the analysis of ritual found in the *Elementary Forms* and the analysis of ritual that is found in the sociology of deviance as seen in Erikson's work. In the analysis of primitive religion ritual was not a variable for Durkheim. All societies were thought to have some form of religious ritual and Durkheim did not propose that the amount of ritual would vary from society to society. In the analysis of deviance on the other hand, if we assume that the community creates deviance, and that the community creation of deviance is essentially a ritualistic activity, then the ritualistic activity of creating deviance becomes a variable. Erikson, for example, was concerned with those situations in which the community suddenly experienced a rapid increase in deviance. This was brought about by a rapid increase in the activity of social control institutions. Conceptualizing ritual as a variable, we now need to explain why some societies have more ritual than others. Erikson explained this variation in the amount of ritualistic activity as a response to some collective crisis in the community, some threat to the community's moral boundaries for which the apprehension of deviants acted to reestablish. My concern though, is with rates of political deviance *across societies*, not with the sudden increase or decrease of a rate within any one society. The answer to explaining these differences among societies, therefore, does not lie in analyzing the kinds of threat that could occur, but with the sociology of religion and particularly the analysis of the function religious ritual performs. It is there that ritual activity is a variable and it is there that the answer to the question of what role ritual plays in creating political deviance can be found.

Sacred-Profane and Deviant-Normal: The Ritual Significance of Creating Political Deviance

As Durkheim noted in the *Elementary Forms*, there is a direct relationship between community rites and the collective representations to which they are performed. Rites, among other things, act to symbolically divide the world into that which is sacred and that which is profane. In doing this, community rituals periodically reaffirm the very sacredness of the symbolic objects in question. By defining that which is sacred or profane, its opposite is automatically defined. In Durkheim's classic analysis of religious rites, whether they be positive or negative rites, they organize the demeanor of individuals in the presence of sacred things. These rites act to create the sense of the sacred, for by defining that which is dirty or impure as opposed to that which is sacred, clean, or pure, this symbolic division acts to periodically reaffirm and redefine that which is sacred and that which is profane.

The community creation of political subversives, whether through trials, rectification campaigns, congressional investigations, or accusations by political authorities, is a ritual practice similar to traditional religious rites. The ritual function is the same. The community creation of political deviance performs the same symbolic classification that religious rites performed: *Instead of dividing things into sacred and profane, the community creation of deviance divides the world into that which is normal and that which is deviant*. The action of the community in creating political deviance performs the same function that religious rituals do in dividing the world into that which is sacred and that which is profane. The similarity between the symbolic classification of sacredness and profanity and that of deviance and normality is quite striking. For instance, just as the sacred is thought to originate from another world, so are deviants thought to exist outside the bounds of normal moral society. Similarly contact with sacred things is prohibited, and deviants, both through the label that is attached and more literally by placing them in prisons, jails, or hospitals, are kept from the more general society. The point is that these ritual separations, in creating sacredness or deviance, automatically creates the other, profanity or normality. Political deviance may be considered in some sense either analogous to the profane or to the sacred. The distinction is irrelevant. What is important is that virtually all aspects of social life can be so categorized and ritually classified.

This ritual classification performs the same function in modern national societies that religious rites and their classifications perform for more traditional or primitive societies. Just as religious rites function to dramatize the presence of those collective representations of more traditional societies, so does the ritual creation of political deviance function to dramatize and create those collective representations of the modern nation state. *In effect, as the sacred requires profanity, so do ideas of what constitutes a country's national interest require the presence of elements that would oppose them.* Just as purity requires dirt for its very existence, so do political ideas of national interest require those that would undermine them to periodically dramatize their very meaning.[10]

The Modern Nation-State: Its Corporate Capacity and Collective Representations

Before continuing with our analysis of the creation of political deviance in the ritual reaffirmation of the central values or collective representations of the modern state, we need to make some assumptions about nation-states as corporate entities.

In line with Weber's (1947) notion of corporate groups, we will deal with the modern state in its distinctly corporate capacity. As political sociologists have noted (Bendix, 1968), the state is a unique institution of modern society, possessing its own set of interests and purposes independent of the interests of its constituent groups and individuals. The state, as Sutton (1959:1) observed, provides the "structures and symbols that permit the whole system to be represented over against its individual members and sub-groups, or outside groups and individuals." When we refer to the interest of the community or the creation of deviance by the community, we will be referring specifically to the apparatus of the state.

What we commonly refer to as government will be conceived of as representing the structural agency through which the corporate capacity of the state is realized. That is, government provides the apparatus for making collective decisions and taking collective action. This understanding of government as the agency for the modern political community is found in Swanson's (1971:611) discussion of the corporate capacity of all social collectivities where corporateness is contained "(a) in a legitimated procedure through which participants can undertake collective action, and (b) a legitimated sphere of action to which the procedures may apply—a sphere of jurisdiction."

Since Durkheim's seminal analysis in the *Elementary Forms* it has been understood in sociology that social collectivities present themselves to their members through a

---

[10]See Douglas (1966) for a discussion of the ritual functions of pollution rules and ideas of dirt.

variety of symbolic material. As Durkheim noted, "the God of the clan, the totemic principle, can therefore be nothing else than the clan itself, personified and represented to the imagination under the visible form of the animal or vegetables which serves as totem."[11] It is interesting that although we have been aware of the notion of the great God: the people," since the French Revolution, sociologists have not seriously approached the symbol, "the people," as a Durkheimian collective representation of the corporate nation-state. With the rise of the modern state there has simultaneously arisen the experience of "the people" or "the nation," "the masses" or "the Proletariat." All of these symbols are collective representations of the new form of ultimate social authority, the modern corporate state.

As with primitive beliefs, the spirit of "the people" is thought to intervene in the daily affairs of modern social life.[12] The spirit of "the people" watches over political institutions: "public opinion" causes political leaders to resign, as in the case of President Johnson; or "public opinion" is thought to force the Congress to pass civil rights legislation. In all these instances, whether it be bourgeois democratic, communist, or fascist states, there has arisen a sense of "the people" or "the public" which has been experienced as a great *force* in these societies. We traditionally have approached the notion of public opinion as members of modern nation-states, and hence have treated public opinion as a "real" force in our social environment and studied it through opinion polls. In modern national societies individuals describe a force, power, or mana, in their presence which they term public opinion. This is very similar to forces such as ancestor spirits which are experienced in more primitive societies. Just as ancestor spirits symbolize the corporate organization of a hunter-gatherer or traditional social systems, so does the power of public opinion symbolize the organization of the corporate nation-state.

The image of "the people" or of "public opinion" is not the only symbolization of the corporate nature of modern societies; flags, national anthems, and national holidays, also serve as collective representations. Similarly, ideas of national purposes or national security along with any one of a number of political ideologies can form part of the symbolic material through which the corporate state presents itself. As Durkheim noted, collective representation need not be found in material objects such as totems or even in the organic presence of "the people." Collective representations may also be embodied in systems of ideas, such as ideas of "American freedom," "Communism," or "socialist development." This is an important point for, as mentioned earlier, I want to view the community creation of deviance as a ritualistic mechanism for creating and maintaining that which is sacred in social life, and that which is sacred is also the collective representation of that society.

Hence, my theory is predicated upon the idea that the community creation of deviance is another way of creating and maintaining the unique set of collective representations which are a part of national societies.

Subversive Elements as Ritual Opposition

The key theoretical proposition of this study is that the modern nation-state manufactures subversives to create a ritual contrast with its set of collective representations.

---

[11]Durkheim (1965:236)
[12]For a discussion of the spirits and gods of primitive societies see Guy E. Swanson, *The Birth of the Gods* (Ann Arbor: University of Michigan Press, 1964).

The function of creating this symbolic contrast with images of collective political purposes is precisely to dramatize and reaffirm the very meaning of these images of the corporate political state. Nation-states are no different from primitive societies in periodically renewing the central meaning of group life. Where community rites reaffirmed the meaning of the symbols of the tribe, they now reaffirm the symbolizations of the modern state.

What is central in this process is the creation of deviants who stand in opposition to the collective representations of the nation itself. As mentioned earlier, these collective representations can take different substantive forms. Subversives can be undermining the "people," the "nation," or a particular ideology. The creation of opposition to the nation and all that it stands for can be accomplished in a number of different ways.

Ideological Opposition. A nation can create ideological deviance by labeling individuals rightists, ultra-leftists, Trotskyites, Titoites, reactionaries or counterrevolutionaries as is done in Communist states. These deviants are, by definition, in opposition to the central ideology of their respective countries and this provides the necessary contrast with the nation's collective purposes. While most pronounced in socialist states, ideological opposition can be manufactured in other kinds of political systems.

Attacking or Undermining National Security. Deviance can also be defined in terms of individuals who are purportedly attacking or undermining the security of the nation. These include such political deviants as wreckers, saboteurs, traitors, or spies. By viewing ideas of what constitutes national security as a set of ideas which can function as a Durkheimian collective representation, the ritual creation of those who attack or subvert these interests provides a symbolic contrast with these images of the corporate state.

Loyalty to the Nation. Another way of creating the ritual opposition is the question of loyalty. Parsons (1955:218) in his analysis of McCarthyism observed that "readiness to make a commitment to a collective interest is a focus of what we ordinarily mean by 'loyalty.' " The accusation of disloyalty by such agencies as the House on Un-American Activities dramatizes the very meaning of loyalty and hence the very meaning of the collective interest.

Personal Interests vs. Collective Interests. A final example involves the ritual distinction between personal or private interests and collective interests. This distinction, while similar to the question of loyalty, has been most dramatically found in China, particularly during the Cultural Revolution. The crimes of "economism" and the problem of being "red and expert" provide good examples.

Economism refers to the purported separation of economic issues from their larger political significance, and more specifically, giving primacy to the working of price mechanisms and material incentives. During a strike in Shanghai, for instance, workers who were seeking higher wages were told they had been "hoodwinked" into following the evil road of "economism" and were "pursuing only personal and short term interests" (Bridgham 1968:9). Accusations of economism by political authorities function to contrast the collective purposes of "building socialism" and "serving the people" with the personal interests of higher wages. The effect of this issue was to dramatize the meaning of such collective purposes as building socialism by the creation of its very opposite, "bourgeois-interest."

The problem of being Red and Expert provides another example of a ritual contrast which occurred during the Chinese Cultural Revolution. Such purposes as "national construction" require not merely the presence of technical skill, being an "expert," but also the proper ideological commitment, to hold the "ideology of collectivism" and to place one's skills "wholeheartedly at the service of the people." Those who are not "red" but merely "expert" do not offer themselves "to the people in socialist construction," but think instead in terms of "individual narrow interests" (Lee, 1966; 1955). Here the corporate purposes of "national construction" are ritually contrasted with their opposite—"individual narrow interests." These examples from China illustrate the myriad forms which this ritual classification can take. What they all share in common is the separation of collective purposes from anything which might oppose them. The most prominent mode of opposition has been the question of individual interests vs. the interests of the nation as a whole.

The Distribution of Political Deviance Through the Social Structure

The corporate state periodically renews itself by defining the presence of subversives who oppose its central values. These political deviants are not created at large within the society but are discovered within certain institutional areas. Not all nations find the same institutional areas infected, and the question remains why some societies find more institutional areas polluted with political subversives than others. We have argued that the creation of deviance is a ritual mechanism for renewing symbolizations of the corporate state. Now, if these symbolizations were infused into or immanent within certain institutional areas, we should expect the ritualistic discovery of deviance in just those areas. This process whereby images of collective purposes come to be distributed throughout everyday life is referred to in the sociology of religion as immanence.

Political Immanence: The Infusion of Ultimate Purposes into Everyday Life

Swanson (1964; 1967) in his study of the religious belief of primitive societies and of the Protestant Reformation suggests that there is a direct relationship between the organization of a society as a corporate actor and the distribution of the symbols of that corporate capacity within the social structure of the community. What is referred to as immanence within the sociology of religion is the situation where the collective representations of the society come to be directly experienced as present within the things and structure of a society. As Swanson notes:

The experience is that of the manner in which God—or other things people find of ultimate importance—are believed to be present in the world of men, nature, and society. In some societies people discover that what they believe of highest value is itself incorporated, is immanent, in persons, organizations, or various objects in the natural world.[13]

For instance, in highly immanent societies, such as the Catholic countries studied by Swanson (1967), the church is considered the mystical body of Christ, and the eucharistic bread and wine, the body and blood of Christ. In Protestant countries, which have a low degree of immanence, ultimate values, such as notions of God, are not incorporated into the things and structure of everyday life. God exists in a transcendent fashion; his essence is not infused into either the organization of the Protestant church or into such material objects as the communion bread and wine.

---

[13]Swanson (1967:1)

Nation-states can also be categorized in terms of their degree of immanence. Collective representations, such as images of "the people" or "the masses" may exist in a transcendent fashion, much like the Protestant God, being all powerful and yet not incorporated into the world they supposedly created. The "American people" are understood to be the origins of our present institutions of government, continually guarding over them, and also the source of political virtue and justice. Although the "American people" remain a force of tremendous power they are not incorporated into those institutions of government they have created. The "people" or "public" as an organic entity is understood to exist independent of political institutions, and each is felt to possess their own set of purposes and goals. The public, or public opinion can, in effect, stand against agents of government; the public can oppose the President, the Congress or the Courts.

In socialist states the "people," "proletariat," or "masses" are similarly understood as the creators of political institutions and as the source of virtue and justice—in Mao's famous words, "The people, and the people alone, are the motive force in the making of world history." But the 'Proletarian will' is embodied within, or immanent within, the actions of the Communist party.[14] Here an organization can embody the collective purposes of the whole society. The actions of the party are also the actions of the "people," whereas in a less immanent society, such as the United States, a "public" and a government are each understood to be capable of independent action and each possesses separate purposes.

One of the more obvious indicators of immanence is the presence of charismatic leaders who embody the will of their people. Recent charismatic leaders, Castro, Nkrumah, Mao, Stalin, are all understood within their societies to, in some fashion, embody the collective purposes of their nation. This infusion of political puposes into political leaders has been commented on before, although not as an example of immanence. What is referred to as a politicized society in the literature of economic and political development is just such a situation. Collective purposes have been observed to be immanent within the political elite of modernizing nations, constituting a situation where "a leader's individual qualities become identified with the collective purposes of an entire nation" (Rustow, 1967). Similarly, Lipset's (1963) analysis of the United States as the "first new nation" referred to national leaders being considered in their society as the "symbol of the new nation, its hero who embodies in his person its values and aspirations." Apter (1963),in his discussion of political religion and new states, similarly speaks of how "many leaders are charismatic who represent the 'one.' They personify the monistic quality of the system." These societies where leaders are seen as embodying the larger collective purposes of their nation are usually described as being highly politicized. This, though, is but another way of saying they are highly immanent.

Because of the long association of the concept of charisma with Weber, it is not ordinarily seen as an instance of immanence. For Weber charisma was more a personal attribute of the leader that was derived from his performance of miraculous deeds: "above all, however, his divine mission must 'prove' itself . . . If he wants to be a prophet, he must perform miracles; if he wants to be a warlord, he must perform heroic deeds."[15] But a Durkheimian interpretation of charisma is also present in Weber's writings: "By its

---

[14]For an interesting discussion of the infusion of ultimate political puposes into social structure see Benjamin Schwartz, "The Reign of Virtue: Some Broad Perspectives on Leader and Party in the Cultural Revolution." *The China Quarterly* 35(July-September 1968):1-17.
[15]Weber (1946:249)

very nature, the existence of charismatic authority is specifically unstable. The holder may forego his charisma; he may feel 'forsaken by his God,' as Jesus did on the cross; he may prove to his followers that 'virtue has gone out of him.' "[16] The notion of "virtue has gone out of him" is very similar to ideas of immanence where larger purposes and meanings can reside in the things of this world, including individuals. Weber thought that charisma was essentially noninstitutional in character, as opposed to rational legal authority which derived from a set of bureaucratic rules, or patrimonial authority which derived from traditional customs.

We can, so to speak, turn Weber on his head by giving a Durkheimian interpretation to charisma. The specific quality of charismatic leaders, their larger than life image, is not derived from the kinds of acts they perform, or from the needs of their followers to create an imaginary supernatural hero. Rather, these properties are symbolizations of group structure and are, under certain conditions, found immanent within certain individuals, roles, or even organizations—as where the communist party is often felt to embody the purposes of the Soviet people. Charisma can derive from the character of society; it need not be solely an individual "personality" attribute as initally suggested by Weber. When the purposes and meanings of the larger social order become immanent we find charismatic leaders.

Other examples of immanence would include societies where moral incentives are understood to be replacing material ones, as in the "red and expert" issue within China. In this situation the performance of institutional roles is understood to be for the larger political purposes of "serving the nation" rather than the individual purposes of personal advancement or material incentives. Larger purposes can also infuse definitions of affect, a situation Inkeles (1968) refers to as the "nationalization of affect." Just as role performance is for a larger collective purpose of "building the nation," so can the meaning of love, hate, desire, or ambition be infused with political significance. Inkeles observes (1968:78):

> You don't have children for the pleasure they give you, but so that Hitler and Mussolini may have more workers and soldiers to effect the high purposes for which they were put on earth. Friendship is not for the gratification it gives, but because comrades may join in carrying out the greatest task of all.

Finally, and perhaps the most dramatic recent example of immanence, was the image of "the thought of Chairman Mao" which had become extensively infused into virtually all aspects of Chinese life (Bergesen, 1978). "Mao's thought" had provided new goals for universities, industrial organizations, and agricultural communes, and individuals possessed by "Mao's thought" had claimed super human efforts, whether learning to fly airplanes, performing medical operations, or playing Ping-Pong (Lifton 1968; Myrdal and Kessle, 1970; Urban, 1971).

The Reaffirmation of Immanent Collective Representations

It has been argued that for modern nation-states ideas of national purposes, national security, images of the people, the nation, or specific tenets of ideologies, such as "building socialism" or "building the nation," can be considered Durkheimian collective representations. These are the cultural objects whereby the presence of the larger

---

[16]Weber (1946:249)

social order is made known to individual members of modern states.

If these collective representations are immanent in or infused into the meaning of everyday life, then their periodic reaffirmation will entail the creation of their ritual opposition, subversive elements, in just the institutional areas in which they are embedded. This is the key theoretical assumption of this study. The creation of deviance is essentially a ritualistic activity and the function of that ritualistic activity is to reaffirm those symbols of corporate life, which in the case of nation-states are the variety of symbolic material ranging from images of people through specific tenets of political ideologies. When these symbols and images can be located within or infused into the structure of everyday life, as in pre-modern society Christ was immanent within the body of the church, then the Durkheimian reaffirmation of these symbolizations will involve the ritual discovery of deviance in different institutional areas. Since collective representations can be located within the structure of everyday life, their ritual reaffirmation will also surround the structures of everyday life. In more highly immanent societies there will be discovered a larger volume of deviance in more institutional sectors than in less immanent societies. This is the central empirical hypothesis of this study.

"Communists" are created within the state department to dramatize the political purposes contained within that structure; "enemies of the people" are discovered within industrial plants to dramatize that the purpose of productive activity is to "build socialism"; and "those taking the capitalist road" are found within the party, universities, military facilities, and on the smallest agricultural commune, to dramatize that the goal and purpose of these organizations is to "serve the people."

The question now is to explain the differential distribution of these collective purposes within different societies. The ritual creation of deviance is a means of reaffirmation of these symbolizations and if we can account for their differential distribution, we can thereby account for the differential distribution of deviance, allowing us to explain why societies like the United States discover political deviance within only a few institutions while other societies, such as China and the Soviet Union, discover deviance in many more institutional areas.

Corporate Organization and the Distribution of Political Deviance

Swanson (1971:621) has argued that the organization of a collectivity as a corporate actor is directly related to the extent to which collective purposes and symbols of that corporate reality will be immanent within the things and structure of that society. Specifically, he hypothesizes that:

> Corporate purposes and choices are more likely to be experienced as present and compelling in the acts of those societies in which the constitutional system—the collective apparatus for making authoritative choices—provided a legitimate role for corporate interests and traditions in the formulation of action, at the same time excluding the special interests and traditions of component groups and individuals in the society.

By considering government as the apparatus for making collective decisions for the corporate state, and categorizing nations in terms of their inclusion of the interests of the country as a whole into this apparatus, we can predict the extensiveness of immanence and hence the extensiveness of the ritually created deviance which functions to reaffirm these immanent collective purposes.

Party Systems: The Incorporation of Group Interests into the National Government

Modern nation-states offer a particular advantage when it comes to classifying their constitutional systems, that is, their "collective apparatus for making authoritative choices." For in the very process of their development these societies had to face and resolve our central theoretical concern: to what extent should various constituent interests be given a formal role in the making of collective decisions. In effect, the very process termed "state formation and nation building" (Bendix, 1969; Rokkan, 1970) represents a movement toward constituting modern societies as corporate actors with the modern state representing the agency endowed with the authority to take legitimate collective action.

Most contemporary societies are constituted as nation-states, regardless of their level of social or economic development, and most nation-states organize their politics through some form of party system. Whether one thinks of the developing nations in Africa, Asia, or Latin America, the socialist states, Russia and China, the past fascist and Nazi polities, or the plural party systems of Anglo-America and Europe, the political party is, as La Palombara and Weiner (1966) comment, "omnipresent." Students of political parties also seem to agree that one of the most important functions of parties is organizing the interests of the populace and representing them within governmental structures. The relationship between various constituent groups and political institutions is mediated by parties.[17]

In a sense, then, party systems are expressions of constitutional systems representing different ways of allowing constituent or corporate interests to penetrate the agency authorized for making collective decisions—the national government.

A Typology of Constitutional Systems

The following is a classification of constitutional systems in terms of the extent to which constituent group interests are given a *formal role* in collective decision making.

Multi-party systems. Multi-party political systems represent the most extensive incorporation of constituent interests into the apparatus for making collective decisions. By definition, multi-party systems allow different group interests, whether they be agricultural, working class, or religious, a position within the national government. Multi-party systems also have an electoral arrangement known as proportional representation, the analysis of which provides an understanding of the manner in which different interests are incorporated. Proportional representation, hereafter referred to as "PR," is an electoral procedure worked out at the beginning of the nineteenth century which attempts to insure a correspondence between the proportion of votes a party receives and the number of seats in the national legislature awarded that party. The electoral arrangements we are concerned with refer to means for selecting representatives to national legislatures and parliaments. There are numerous specific formulas that have been devised but these are not of interest here.[18] Proportional representation is indicative of the incorporation of constituent interests into a central decision making apparatus because each party, no matter what share of the vote it receives, will be assigned exactly the same share of legislative seats. That is, if one receives only 5 percent of the vote, one is still represented with 5 percent of the seats. If one receives 50

---

[17]See Almond and Powell (1966), Kirkheimer (1966), Lipset (1960), Rokkan (1966).
[18]See Raye (1971), Rokkan (1968)

percent of the vote, one is given 50 percent of the seats. This is in direct contrast to a plurality system in which the winner takes all the seats. The party that received only 5 percent of the vote would get no seats. The party that received 50 percent of the vote would get all the seats.

The emergence of PR systems was in response to three crises involving the prospective role of different constituent interests in the newly emerging unified national legislatures during the nineteenth century.

First, in the process of nation-building, some of the most ethnically heterogenous European countries found entrenched linguistic, ethnic, or religious minorities threatening to disrupt the emerging national community, if majority representation, which would deny their representation, persisted. Hence, some of the most heterogenous countries were the first to adopt proportional representation: Denmark in 1855, the Swiss Cantons in 1891, Belgium in 1899, Moravia in 1905, Finland in 1906.[19] The construction of nation-states involves working on institutional arrangements determining how corporate authority was to be exercised, with particular attention being paid to the role various types of groups were to play. As Rokkan further commented, the introduction of PR played an important role in the "strategy of territorial consolidation and national integration," for by giving these groups a role in decision making the unity of the collectivity was preserved, providing "an alternative to monopolization of influence or civil war."

A second crisis occurred when the extension of suffrage to ever widening circles of the populace led to the development of strong lower-class parties which desired representation in national legislatures. The majority principle, though, often placed the barrier against entry so high that many new parties found it difficult to enter the legislature. The German rule of absolute majority established the highest barrier for entering—having to obtain 50 percent of the vote or go without representation. This led working class parties to push for the adoption of PR systems, which would more easily allow them to gain representation.

Finally, given the pressure from growing working class parties, older bourgeois parties felt threatened by their growing strength and to protect their position "demanded PR to protect their position against the new wave of mobilized voters created by universal suffrage."[20]

In all three cases whether to give representation to religious or ethnic interests, to working class interests, or to protect the interests of older parties, PR represents a form of constitutional system where group interests (in the form of Catholic, agrarian, or working class parties) are given a formal role in the making of collective decisions. The very presence of these parties, almost regardless of what percentage of the popular vote they command, insures them a role through the proportion of seats they receive.

Two-party system. The second category in our scheme of constitutional systems is represented by two-party states, which include both majority and plurality electoral arrangements. Since the majority formula is rarely used, we will discuss plurality systems as a way of understanding the constitutional system found with two party systems. Plurality or simple majority electoral arrangements found in two party systems require that the party obtain more votes than its nearest competitor to win an election. This type of electoral arrangement is associated with the Anglo-American states of New Zealand, Australia, Britain, and the United States.

Two-party systems with the plurality formula as the basis for selecting members to

---

[19]Rokkan (1968)
[20]Rokkan (1968:12)

national legislatures and parliaments, allow various component interests within the nation a less formal voice than with proportional representation in multi-party systems. The requirement of winning an election provides an advantage to larger parties and prevents smaller ones, who represent more specific interest or ideological perspectives, from being represented. Therefore, in contrast with multi-party systems, where a party is assured that its special interests will be present regardless of its electoral showing, plurality systems can be said to allow less penetration of consituent interests.

The important dimension of constitutional systems is not the mere inclusion or exclusion of constituent interests, but the corresponding inclusion of public interests. In this regard two-party systems involve a greater inclusion of corporate interests than do multi-party systems for the following reasons.

The requirement of winning an election in order to gain entrance to the legislature places pressure upon parties to appeal to the various groupings which may not regularly share the perspective of the party. Appealing to or representing the interests of one single group is not sufficient to win elections, and parties appeal to the *common* interests of the community. The interests and purposes which various groups *share* is what is represented, rather than those interests specific to each group.[21]

Two party systems also represent the interests of politically defined groups, such as states, counties, cities, and electoral districts. For instance, in the United States questions of interest representation are defined in terms of the interests of the "people of California," or the "citizens of Santa Clara County," rather than stratificational dimensions of class, wealth, or prestige and ascriptive solidarities such as race, religion, or ethnic creed. The point is not that these dimensions are not factors in elections or that issues are not defined in these terms, but that one participates in collective decision making (some form of legislature) representing the interests of a politically defined community. One represents New York, Florida, or the 17th district; one is not formally authorized to represent solely the interests of Catholics, Protestants, workers, or farmers.

We have moved from societies where constituent interests were given a maximum amount of influence within the structure for collective decision making to nations where broader interests crossing the interests of numerous specific groups are formally incorporated into central decision making. Our final category represents a constitutional arrangement where only corporate interests are present, and constituent interests are formally excluded.

One-Party Systems. Single party states, whether socialist, fascist, or nationalist, because there is only one party representing the interests of the society as a whole, should be the most immanent (politicized). One-party states can be broken into two general categories. First, prior to the onrush of new nations following the Second World War, single-party states associated with Nazi Germany, Fascist Italy, and Communist Russia, were depicted in terms of terror, purges, and total control—the classic totalitarian society. With the advent of new states after the war, particularly in Africa,[22] one-party states were increasingly described in terms of their functions for facilitating modernization. These states were now characterized as "mobilizational," "revolutionary-centralizing," or "revolutionary mass-movement regimes."[23]

---

[21]Lipset (1960)
[22]Hodgkin (1961); Schachter (1961); Kilson (1963); Wallerstein (1966).
[23]Banks and Texter (1963); Coleman and Rosburg (1964); Tucker (1961).

By definition, in single-party states there is only one interest represented in the central agency entrusted with collective action. This is the national interest, the corporate interest of the nation as a collective actor.

The party often takes over the role of making collective decisions, which is usually left to government. The party acts both as the representative of interests of the nation as a whole, and as the agency for carrying out those interests and purposes. This is a function performed by political parties that is not found in either multi-party or two-party systems, although two-party systems come closer to representing the interests of the whole than do multi-party systems.

Ritual Government Actions and the Creation of Political Subversives

Political deviants are created by the social definitions and labels of deviancy the community can apply. Although it has traditionally been understood that deviant labels are applied by social-control institutions such as police, prisons, or hospitals, labels of deviance can also be generated and applied by institutions other than those formally chartered functions of social control. In line with Goffman's (1965) idea that the construction of social definitions can be accomplished by numerous ritual activities, we will include the actions of political authorities as the principal source of deviance labels.

As mentioned earlier, government authorities are formally constituted agents for the larger society, and in this capacity they act for that community in defining the meaning of political subversion. This social construction of deviance can be accomplished in at least three general fashions.

Ritual accusations. The simplest mode of defining the presence of subversives, counter-revoluationaries, reactionaries, spies, or espionage rings is the mere statement that they exist. They would include Senator McCarthy's claim that there were "X" number of communists in the State Department, or the claim by Chinese political elites that "class enemies" have "sneaked into our ranks" and are "plotting capitalist restoration" and "infecting our minds with bourgeois ideas." In effect, any statement, speech, or press release offered by constituted political authorities to the effect that subversive elements exist, or that the nation is somehow endangered, constitutes a ritual mechanism for defining the presence of subversion.

Traditional social control mechanisms. The definitional power of the community is greatly enhanced over mere accusations by the actions of formally constituted agencies of social control. Activities by police, courts, imprisonment, deportation, or the passage of new restrictions, are all traditional control mechanisms that can be employed to define the presence of political subversives.

Community ceremonies. Finally, the community can convene itself in the form of political trials and investigations, such as the Stalinist show trials and the McCarthy Army Hearings. These activities involve the most extensive use of ritual embellishment of all the mechanisms at the disposal of the state. Trials with their ritual confessions, self-criticisms, elaborate accusations, and extensive media coverage provide unsurpassed public drama. The employment of censorship campaigns or rectification campaigns, where the community makes extensive efforts to cleanse itself of subversive elements, is a further, large-scale, community effort which functions to ritually define the presence of deviants.

In short, the state possesses a great variety of ritual mechanisms for defining the presence of subversive activity and for labeling individuals as political deviants. All of these activities have, at one time or another, been employed to create the sense of internal danger or threats to national security.

A Model of the Witch-Hunting Process

The theoretical argument that images of national purposes can be immanent within the things and structure of a community, and that political authorities create subversives in the very structures that are infused with political significance as a means of reaffirming these larger political purposes, can be represented in the following causal model.

FIGURE 2-1

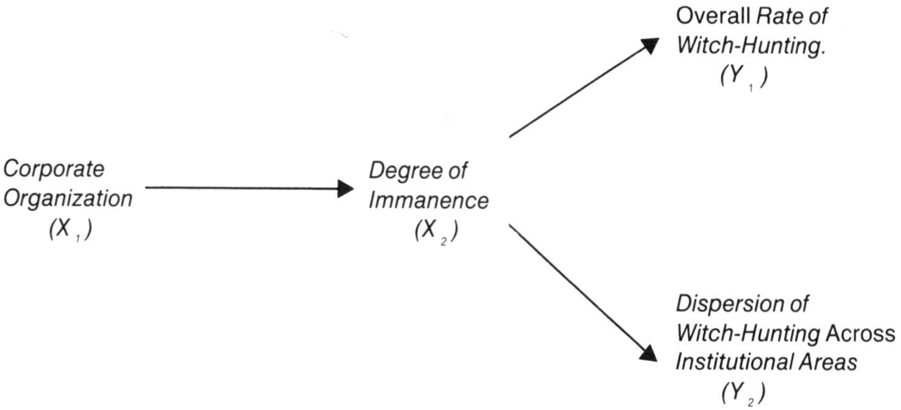

Corporate Organization (X_1) → Degree of Immanence (X_2) → Overall *Rate of Witch-Hunting.* (Y_1)

Degree of Immanence (X_2) → *Dispersion of Witch-Hunting Across Institutional Areas* (Y_2)

Hypotheses

From this model the following hypotheses can be derived:
(i) The greater the inclusion of corporate interests at the expense of constituent interests in the structure for making collective decision (X_1), the greater the overall rate of witch-hunting (Y_1).
(ii) The greater the inclusion of corporate interest at the expense of constituent interests in the structure for making collective decisions (X_1), the greater the dispersion of witch-hunting (Y_2).

Conclusion

This formulation of political deviance suggests that the origins of deviance need not be considered solely as a response to some type of crisis. Political deviance has its origins in the very organization of collectivities as corporate actors. Similarly, deviance need no longer be viewed as functioning solely to repair problematical social boundaries. Deviance also serves to reaffirm that which is stable and enduring in social life—the corporate nature of all national societies. Finally, this theory allows for the comparative analysis of political witch-hunts, and as such provides an advancement over the previous piecemeal treatment they have been given. I have provided a general formulation that is not limited to the specific institutional properties of selected nations, but can be applied cross-nationally to a large sample of societies. This formulation also expands the understanding of witch-hunts from being previously considered as an institutional feature solely of totalitarian states to being a generalized social ritual employed by all societies to periodically reaffirm their corporate existence.

CHAPTER 3
METHODOLOGY

In this chapter I will discuss the research design necessary to test the hypotheses advanced in Chapter 2. The hypotheses of linking the organization of nation states as corporate entities, and hence their relative degree of immanence, with the overall rate of deviance and the dispersion of political deviance through these countries' social structures, requires the measurement of three variables: (a) corporate organization, (b) the overall rate of witch-hunting and (c) the dispersion of that witch-hunting through the social structure. The measurement of corporate organization will be accomplished by characterizing each nation in our sample according to its party system. To measure rates of witch-hunting the technique of "event analysis," devised by students of civil disorders and political violence (see Tilly and Rule, 1965; Snyder and Tilly, 1972; Feierabend and Feierabend, 1966, 1969; Gurr, 1968) will be employed. This data gathering technique involves coding the occurrence of political events from news sources such as the *New York Times*. This technique has traditionally been employed to code the presence of riots, assassinations, coups, and other forms of political violence, but it will be utilized here to code the occurrence of government events that ritually define the presence of political subversives, such as trials, investigations, arrests, deportations, and accusations. This procedure allows the gathering of information that is not available from traditional sources of cross-national data, such as the *U.N. Yearbook*, or the *Europa Yearbook*. The measurement of the dispersion of witch-hunting through each nation's social structure will be accomplished through the creation of a Deviance Distribution Index, based upon the population diversity indexes employed in demographic and ecological research (see Duncan and Duncan, 1955; or Lieberson, 1969).

Both tabular and multiple regression analysis will be employed to analyze the data on the overall rate of witch-hunting and the dispersion of the deviance the witch-hunting creates through the social structure. The tabular analysis will be used to show the overall rates and dispersion index scores for each country in the sample. The multivariate analysis will involve our independent variable, party system, along with a series of control variables to insure that the relationship between party systems and rates and dispersion of witch-hunting is not spurious.

Period of Observation

I am not interested in any specific outbreak of witch-hunting such as the McCarthy period or the Cultural Revolution, but rather with the average rate of witch-hunting experienced by a nation. To code the data a period of observation was selected. A long period would be optimal to negate the bias that comes from shorter periods where the presence of a particular outburst of witch-hunting would bias the score for that country. That is, if I chose the years 1940 through 1950, the United States, in the midst of the McCarthy period would receive a much higher score than if I coded from 1950 to 1970. The 1940s were preoccupied with war which provides data, such an additional set of variables that I did not want to consider my simplified model. The period of observation chosen was that between 1950 and 1955.

Indicators of Corporate Organization: Political Party Systems

The unit of analysis for this study is the sovereign nation-state, no colonies or territories are included. The indicator of the organization of a nation-state as a corporate entity will be that country's system of political parties. While a random sample of one-party, two-party, and multi-party systems would have been optimal, important theoretical concerns and operational difficulties presented constraints in the choice of a sample of nations. The central theoretical assertion of this monograph concerns the organization of nations as corporate entities with the state providing the structural apparatus for taking collective action.

My sample of multi-party and two-party states is taken from Blondel's (1968) study of party systems and government stability. Blondel created his sample by looking at the average percent of the popular vote in national elections that went to the two major parties. This average two-party vote was computed between 1945 and 1966, and provides an empirically based procedure for separating two-party and multi-party systems.

Most of the one-party states are socialist countries, but as mentioned previously, the other principal source of one-party states, the African one-party nations, were not as yet independent during my period of observation.[24]

The sample of nations included in this study are the following:

One-Party States	
China	New Zealand
Czechoslovakia	Australia
East Germany	Great Britain
Hungary	
Poland	*Multi-Party States*
Yugoslavia	
U.S.S.R.	Belgium
Rumania	Ireland
Bulgaria	Denmark
Albania	Iceland
Mexico	Norway
	Sweden
Two-Party States	Finland
	France
U.S.A.	Netherlands
	Switzerland
	Italy

---

[24]Mexico is included, although it is technically a one-party dominant state. That is, one major party has dominated Mexican politics, although there are other small parties which occupy some seats in the national legislature. But, because this system is closer to a one-party state than either two-party or multi-party, it was coded as a one-party state.

Measuring the Rate of Witch-Hunting

Data on the rate of witch-hunting were gathered through a technique know as "event analysis" which has been developed by students of civil violence and political disorder to obtain data which is not normally accessible for cross-national research. There is a variety of sources from which political events can be coded. Gurr (1968) in his study of political violence used the *New York Times, Newsyear, African Diary: Weekly Record of Events in Africa*, and the *Hispanic-American Report.* The Feierabends (1969) in their study of civil disorders and political violence gathered data from *Deadline Data On World Affairs*, and the *Encyclopedia Britannica Yearbook.* Preliminary examination of these different news sources suggests that the *New York Times* (through its *Index*) provides the most comprehensive coverage of the events I am interested in. This also seems to be the conclusion of other researchers who have relied primarily upon the *Times Index* (Tanter, 1966; Rummel, 1966; Eckstein, 1962; Paige, 1971).

My indicator of the presence of political subversives within a country will come from coding the number of ritual actions taken by the state, through its institutions of social control, in the process of definitionally creating political subversion. That is, when a nation tries a member of the military for subversion, or a congressional committee investigates a professor for Communist leanings, these actions by constituted political authorities will be used as my indicators of the presence of deviance. As the actual number of deviants reported in the press is subject to a high degree of exaggeration and misreporting, this procedure will probably be underestimating the actual number of deviants, since there is a high probability that those ritual actions taken by the government create more than one deviant. Each state act will then be classified in terms of the institutional area where it defines the presence of deviants, thereby providing the necessary information on the institutional location.

The *The New York Times Index* was the source of data for government events. Although the method of event analysis allows for the gathering of data on variables not available elsewhere, there are numerous sources of bias involved both in using press reports as sources of data, and in using one particular paper. Obviously, there are numerous actions taken by political authorities in identifying and prosecuting subversives that never reach the pages of the *Times*. This would seem to be particularly relevant for events that occur in Communist states, and in countries which have little contact with the United States. There is also a bias in terms of the amount of events reported for large and prestigious nations over smaller and less known ones. The larger nations obviously receive more press coverage than smaller nations. Although the *Times* undoubtedly reports more events within the United States than other countries, there is probably less bias across nations than is found within regional presses of any particular area.

Coding Scheme for Government Activities Which Create Political Subversion

Having decided upon the *New York Times* as the source of data, a coding scheme was prepared and applied to this news source. This scheme (see Appendix II for the complete coding scheme) has three basic sections: (1) a category scheme for different kinds of acts the state can take in ritually defining the presence of political deviance, (2) a category scheme of the different institutional areas in which these deviants can be discovered, and (3) other information about the deviants, such as the date on which they are discovered, the types of deviant labels that are applied, and the kind of punishment that is applied.

State Action. The first thing coded was the various actions political authorities take in creating subversion which range from mere verbal accusations to such large scale activities as political trials. The categories of this coding scheme are listed below:

  (1) Warnings of dangers and threats to the nation
  (2) Specific charges of subversion
  (3) The discovery of plots
  (4) Calls for public action to thwart political deviance
  (5) Calls for the support of the nation
  (6) Proposed, pledged, or threatened actions to thwart deviance
  (7) Creation of new laws to check deviance
  (8) Restriction of individual or group activity for political reasons
  (9) Expulsion of agents of a foreign government
(10) Deportations outside a country
(11) Deportations within the country
(12) Arrests
(13) Imprisonment, or being sentenced
(14) Resignations from office for political reasons
(15) Purges
(16) Court Actions defining the presence, or actions to thwart deviance
(17) Issuing subpoenas, indictments, or bringing charges of subversive activity
(18) Mass mobilizations: rectification campaigns, etc.
(19) Censorship campaigns
(20) Openings of major political trials
(21) Sentences following major political trials
(22) Self criticisms, confessions, etc.
(23) Opening of government investigations
(24) Testifying at investigations

Each of these categories is mutually exclusive, the coder can code an event under only one category. The great variety of government events will allow us to examine in future studies the different kinds of actions that are taken in different types of political systems.

Institutional areas. Once an event was identified, and coded, the next step was to code the institutional area in which subversion was discovered. If, for instance, an accusation is made that there are "Communists" in the state department, the institutional area coded would be "the national bureaucracy." In this part of the coding scheme I have created seven different institutional areas:

(1) Government
(2) Political party—only in one-party states
(3) Military institutions
(4) Educational institutions
(5) Professions
(6) Religious institutions
(7) Economic institutions

Within each of these general areas there are a number of more specific statuses, so that, within the educational institutions category one can code events in the categories: university, college, technical school, professor, student. Within political institutions there are categories for executive leadership, representative bodies, national bureaucracy, and local or provincial government. These categories, like the government activities codes, are mutually exclusive. Only one institutional area can be coded for each action taken in the ritualistic creation of political deviance.

Additional Information. Other features of the deviance creation process were coded for future analysis. These include the *level of political authority instigating the ritual action*, which refers to whether it was executive leadership, national bureaucracy, or legislative bodies which made the charges, organized the trials, or instigated the censorship campaigns. This information will allow me to further specify the nature of the deviance creation process. By stratifying levels of political authority I can examine the label generating process in more detail. That is, in which types of political systems and for which types of crime are different levels of political authority utilized in creating and applying deviant labels. I also coded the *type of deviant label* that is applied. Are political deviants accused of subversion, wrecking, or taking the capital road? This type of question can be examined empirically with the data that I have collected, and will be one of the first priorities in any follow-up study. I also have coded the *type of punishment* whenever it is mentioned and the *number of deviants* that are mentioned. This, like the other information, allows for a further analysis into the specifics of deviance creation and the mechanics of conducting political witch-hunts. The final information coded was the *month and year* in which the particular government action was taken and the *code number of the country* being coded. The month and year will allow me to perform longitudinal analysis, dissecting a witch-hunt as it develops. The interrelationships between types of ritual government activity, levels of political authority, and different types of deviant labels can be analyzed as the witch-hunt unfolds. This information will allow me, in effect, to study the "life cycle" of an unfolding political witch-hunt.

Coding Procedures

The coding was accomplished by a group of four graduate students at Stanford University. Before the actual coding began, a preliminary form of the coding scheme was Xeroxed and the group of coders practiced coding a few of the countries within the sample. All coders coded the same country for the same years and then compared their results. Discrepancies amongst the coders were then worked out, and often this involved adding new categories, and coming to inter-subjective agreement as to just what constitutes a particular kind of event. This procedure of coding a common set of countries was continued until a high degree of reliability among the coders was reached, at which point the final form of the coding scheme was Xeroxed and the actual coding began. Reliability checks were performed along the way, and where necessary, the joint coding process continued until a high level of reliability was reached. In the previous research using this coding technique reliability was not a major problem. Gurr (1967) reports an inter-coder correlation of .75 on his five measures of political violence. The Feierabends (1966), in checking the consensual validation of their intensiveness of violence scale, report levels of agreement ranging from .87 to .94 among their coders.

Finally, Banks (1971) reports coefficients of agreement of .97 for a scale of political instability developed by Rummel (1966).

Our coefficient of agreement amongst the four coders was .86.[25]

This reliability score was computed by having the four coders code three countries—France in 1954, Czechoslovakia in 1953, and China in 1965. They coded the government activities code, that is, the extent to which accusations, imprisonment, deportations, etc., were present in creating political deviance. The agreement score represents the agreement amongst these coders as to the total number of accusations, imprisonments, etc., within each of these three countries.

An Illustration of the Coding Procedure. To illustrate how the coding procedure actually operates, consider the following example taken from a section of the *New York Times Index* for Poland in 1953.

Govt protests alleged espionage by US; claims seizure of 2 agents dropped by parachute, Ja 18, 29:4; US Army hdqrs, Ger, denies training and parachuting spies, JA 21,11:2; US rejects Polish charge that US finances subversion, F 10,11:1

2 to be tried as US spies, Warsaw, F 17,12:7; sentenced to death, F 19,5:3; exile S Korbonski holds alleged confession by underground leaders staged by Govt to counter US announcement of liberation policy, F 25,11:5

In coding this the coders would take their coding scheme to the Stanford Library, where the Indexes of the *Times* are located, and would open them to Poland in 1953 and begin coding. The coding is done directly upon IBM Data Assembler Sheets, which can then easily be punched on cards by IBM keypunch operators.

In explaining how this section would be coded, the code number, 01, for instance, refers to the code number on the coding sheet. The column number, 1-2, for instance, refers to the column on the IBM card where the code number is recorded.

In this section there are two events: "Government protests alleged espionage" and "two to be tried as United States spies." The first event, "Government protests alleged espionage," would be coded under "specific charges and accusations" (code 01 in Columns 1-2). Now, once an event has been identified, it is further categorized along a number of dimensions. The level of political authority taking the ritual action in question would be "government in general" (code 01 in columns 3-4), and the characterization of the deviant activity is "espionage" (code 01 in columns 5-6). The remaining categories in the coding scheme are not relevant to this type of event and hence are coded 99, except for the month "January" (code 01 in columns 9-10); the country code (code 135 for Poland in columns 11-12), and the year "53" (columns 22-23).

---

[25]Reliability for our coding scheme was computed using Robinson's (1957) coefficient of agreement, which is based on the following formula:

$$A = 1 - \frac{\Sigma (X_{1j} - \overline{X}_j)^2 + \Sigma (X_{2j} - \overline{X}_j)^2}{\Sigma (X_{1j} - \overline{X}_j)^2 + \Sigma (X_{2j} - \overline{X}_j)^2}$$

In this formula, A = the coefficient of agreement, x^{1j} the score of the second coder for the jth category, and x^{2j} the score of the second coder for the jth category and x^j the mean of the jth category.

The second event, "two to be tried as United States spies," is coded under the event code "tried or sentenced" (code 13 in columns 1-2). Here the level of political authority taking this ritual action is not mentioned, and these cases are coded under "government generally" (code 01 in columns 3-4). The characterization of deviant activity is "treason-spying" (code 01 in columns 5-6); the institutional location of the discovered deviance is code 99 since it is not mentioned. The month "February" (code 02 in columns 9-10); and the "death sentence" mentioned is coded in the punishment section under "death or execution" (code 05 in columns 11-12). The number of deviants is recorded when it is mentioned; in this case there are two (in columns 15-18). Finally, the country code (135 for Poland in columns 19-20), and the year "53" (columns 22-23), are coded.

In this fashion the twenty-six countries in the sample were coded according to the coding scheme presented in the Appendix. The countries were randomly divided among the four coders, and the coding took place at the Stanford Library.

Measuring the Dispersion of Witch-Hunting Throughout the Social Structure

To measure the dispersion of witch-hunting throughout the social structure, Simpson's (1949) Index of Population Diversity was employed. Population diversity indexes were devised to determine the relative diversity or dispersion of a population among a variety of ethnic, racial or linguistic groups. The basic procedure (Lieberson, 1969) is to randomly select pairs of individuals from a population and determine the probability that they share a common group membership. The computation of this index provides an indicator of the relative diversity of the population in relationship to these groups. This technique was adapted to our research problem. Instead of examining the distribution of individuals within linguistic categories, we examine the distribution of a population of deviants within institutional categories. As mentioned earlier, the presence of subversion within these categories was derived from coding the areas in which government activities define deviance, such that trials of school personnel indicate subversion in educational institutions; trials of military personnel indicated subversion in military institutions; and so forth. In this fashion each government action was classified in terms of the institutional area where it ritually defines the presence of a political deviant, providing the necessary information on institutional locations.

A Deviance Distribution Index score was computed for each of the twenty-six nations in our sample and entered as raw data into multiple regression equations containing the independent variable, party system, and a series of control variables.

Control Variables

I entered a series of control variable into the analysis to control for the possibility that the independent variable, party system, may actually be masking the effect of another variable which I have not controlled. For instance, the party system variable may be masking the effect of economic development such that two party and multi-party states are also more economically developed than many one-party states which are in the process of modernization. The relationship between party systems and rates of political deviance may be spurious, hiding the real relationship between level of economic development and rates of deviance. Underdeveloped countries may have trials and political persecutions for the purpose of eliminating aspects of the traditional social order in facilitating development. This argument, for instance, has been generated to account for much of the Soviet terror and trials during the 1930s (Dallin and Breslauer, 1970).

Government Revenue. My indicator of the relative power of the state is government revenue as a proportion of total national income. These data were obtained from the World Tables (1971) of the World Bank. The larger the proportion of a country's GNP extracted by the state, the stronger the state. These data, unfortunately, are not available for socialist countries. Since socialist states constitute the overwhelming majority of the one-party nations, this presents a problem for analysis. The following step was taken to provide an approximation of the values on this variable. There are data on Yugoslavia, which has a score of .332, and using that as a base, the values for all other socialist countries was arbitrarily set at . 350. There exist, obviously, real differences in the amount of government revenue and setting all values at .350 does not capture this difference. The value for Yugoslavia is higher than that for any other country in the sample, and I think we can safely assume that the other values for socialist states would also be higher than those for the other nations. If we assume that many socialist states would have values higher than .350, then we are probably underestimating, rather than overestimating, the real value. The reason for this approximation of government revenue is to allow us to utilize these ten nations in our sample of one-party states, not to accurately assess the real amount of government revenue. For this purpose setting their value at .350 seems a reasonable procedure.

Percent Males in Agriculture. A conventional indicator of economic development used in cross-national research is the percent of economically active males in agriculture as a proportion of the total male working force. Each of the countries in the sample received a score on this variable, which is taken from the ILO Project Series (1971). The greater the percentage of the work force employed in agriculture, the less economically developed the nation.

Ethno-Linguistic Fractionalization. This variable serves as an indicator of the degree of diversity within a nation in terms of ethnic and linguistic groups. The scale is taken from Atlas Narodov Mira (1971) and computed in terms of the following equation: $F = 1 - (N_{subl}/N) (N_{subl} - 1/N - 1)$, where N_{subl} equals the number of people in the Ith group, N equals the total population, and F equals the degree of ethno-linguistic fractionalization. The higher the score on this index, the more heterogeneous a nation in terms of the ethno-linguistic groups which comprise it.

Population. The indicator of the relative size of the country will be data on its population. These data are also taken from the World Tables of the World Bank (1971).

Data Analysis

Now that we have measures of corporate organization, the rate of witch-hunting and the dispersion of witch-hunting through the social structure, along with a series of control variables, we can test our hypotheses. The only variable for which we have no indicators is immanence (X^2), and hence it will go unmeasured. The regression equations for this analysis are:

(i) $Y^1 = a + b^1 X^1 + b^2 X^2 + b^3 X^3 + b^4 X^4 + b^5 X^5 + u$

(ii) $Y^2 = a + b^1 X^1 + b^2 X^2 + b^3 X^3 + b^4 X^4 + b^5 X^5 + u$

Where:

Y^1 = Volume of political deviance

Y^2 = Deviance Dispersion Index

X^1 = Political party system (one-party, two-party, multi-party)

X^2 = Government revenue as a percent of total national income

X^3 = Percent of male workforce actively employed in agriculture

X^4 = Degree of ethno-linguistic fractionalization

u = the error term

CHAPTER 4

CORPORATE ORGANIZATION AND THE OVERALL RATE OF WITCH-HUNTING

This chapter examines the relationship between the organization of nations as corporate entities, as indicated by type of party system, and their overall rate of witch-hunting as indicated by the rate of government actions which ritualistically create political deviance. Because any two variable analysis is always open to the charge that other variables, highly correlated with the independent variable, may in fact be having the principal effect upon the dependent variable, we will utilize a multivariate analysis. The hypothesis concerning corporate organization and rates of witch-hunting will be tested by utilizing multiple regression techniques. Our independent variables include political party systems, our variable of theoretical interest, and the series of control variables discussed in Chapter 3: govenment revenue, percent males in agriculture, ethno-linguistic heterogeneity, and the country's population.

The dependent variable for this analysis is the total number of witch-hunting events between 1950 and 1955. Chapter 3 describes the data gathering procedure and gives a complete list of the different types of government activities coded to generate these data. The ritual actions include some twenty-three different kinds of acts, ranging from accusations and deportations to arrests, imprisonment, and political trials. This variable was logged[26] (Log ^{10}) to give the distribution a less skewed shape, as there were some extreme values on this variable. China, for instance, had a total of 167 events and Czechoslovakia 160, while Belgium had only 5 events, and Norway only 4. Also, the United States with 189 was excluded from this analysis because of the possible bias in the reporting of the *New York Times*. Since there was no way to approximate the actual amount of ritual activity in the United States during this period, it was simply eliminated from this particular analysis.

Findings

Data bearing on the hypothesis postulating a relationship between corporate organization, as indicated by political party system, and rates of political deviance is found in Table 4-1. In this Table the overall number of witch-hunting acts per country is presented. New Zealand, Ireland, and Iceland had no events coded during this period. It is not clear whether this finding is an artifact of the small size of these countries and their relative isolation and distance from metropolitan centers, hence the failure of the *New York Times* to report their activities, or whether they actually experienced no witch-hunting. The possibility of bias in the news reporting of the *Times* is seen in the extraordinary number of events reported for the United States, which received 189 events, a number larger than any other country in the entire sample. This finding is particularly difficult to interpret, for while there was undoubtedly a bias in the reporting,

---

[26]This was performed through an SPSS program.

Table 4-1
TOTAL NUMBER OF WITCH-HUNTING ACTIVITIES
BETWEEN 1950 AND 1955*

Type of Corporate Organization

One-Party		Two-Party		Multi-Party	
China	167	United States	189	France	40
Czechoslovakia	160	Great Britain	41	Finland	11
East Germany	101	Australia	8	Netherlands	11
Hungary	86	New Zealand	0	Denmark	9
Poland	81			Switzerland	9
Yugoslavia	79			Sweden	9
U.S.S.R.	63			Italy	8
Rumania	37			Belgium	5
Bulgaria	25			Norway	4
Albania	9			Ireland	0
Mexico	3			Iceland	0
Mean = 73.9		Mean = 16.3[a] 59.5[b]		Mean = 9.6	
Std. Dev. = 52.1		Std. Dev. = 15.0[a] 75.6[b]		Std. Dev. = 9.4	
Median = 79.0		Median = 8.0[a] 25.5[b]		Median = 9.0	

*The total number of government actions employed in creating deviance is the indicator of the total number of political deviants.

[a]Excluding the United States

[b]Including the United States

the United States was also involved in the McCarthy witch-hunts during this period.

Table 4-1 also presents the average number of witch-hunting activities and from this table we can see that the hypothesis positing a relationship between the organization of nation-states as corporate entities and witch-hunting is supported.

Corporate Organization and Witch-Hunting: A Multivariate Analysis

In this analysis the following variables were entered into a regression equation: number of witch-hunting acts, percent males in agriculture, ethno-linguistic heterogeneity, and population. Our dependent variable, number of witch-hunting acts, was regressed against these independent variables which were all entered simultaneously into the regression equation.[27] Table 4-2 presents the relationship between the set of independent variables and our dependent variable.[28]

Table 4-2
TOTAL NUMBER OF WITCH-HUNTING ACTIVITIES
REGRESSED AGAINST INDEPENDENT VARIABLES

Independent Variables	Dependent Variable: Total Number of			
	B	Beta	Std. Error B	F
Political Party System	.350	.50	.135	6.682
Government Revenue, 1955	.0039	.36	.00171	5.425
Percent Males in Agriculture, 1955	-.00003	-.10	.00007	.259
Ethno-Linguistic Frationalization	.00034	.11	.00048	.483
Population, 1955	.00013	.24	.00009	2.122

Variance Explained (R^2): .60
Number of cases: 25

Note:
Political Party System = Nation characterized by party system: one-party, two-party, multi-party (coded 3, 2, 1).
Government Revenue = Government Revenue as a percent of total national income, from the World Tables (1971).
Percent Males in Agriculture = Percent of male workforce actively employed in agriculture, from ILO Project Series (1971).
Ethno-Linguistic Fractionlization = Degree of ethno-linguistic fractionalization from Atlas Narodov Mira (1971).
Witch-Hunting Activities = Total number of government events defining the presence of political deviance between 1950 and 1955.
Population = Country's population, from World Tables (1971).

---

[27]Regression performed with a program from SPSS.
[28]The correlation matrix for these variables can be found in Appendix I. Although the F-ratio is presented, its use for determining statistical significance makes no sense here as we are not sampling from a large population of countries, or generalizing these findings to such a larger population.

Inspecting Table 4-2 we can see that the hypothesis positing a direct link between the organization of a country as a corporate entity and the number of witch-hunting activities is supported. The party system variable, our indicator of corporate organization with a beta of .50, is dramatically larger than that for any of our other independent variables.

The variable percent males in agriculture with a beta of -.10 represents a slight positive relationship between economic development and number of witch-hunting acts. This relationship, though is so small that there seems to be no substantive relationship between the extent of economic development and the propensity to experience witch-hunts.

The relationship of ethno-linguistic heterogeneity (beta .11) is similar to the economic development variable, in that there is a very slight positive relationship with the amount of witch-hunting. Although this relationship is quite small, its substantive interpretation is important in that it does not lend support to a group conflict interpretation of political trials or purges. That is, in nations which have diverse ethnic or linguistic groups, tensions and hostilities between them could be reflected in the use of the state apparatus by one group to persecute the other. Charges of espionage, treason, and crimes against the state could be a mechanism whereby one group suppresses and dominates the other. Our small finding, though, does not lend support to this interpretation.

Population, as an indicator of the size of a country, with a beta of .24, indicates that independent of the way in which a nation is organized there is a slight positive relationship between its size and the number of witch-hunting activities. Although this is a positive relationship, it is, though, not as large or significant as the party variable. This is another important finding in that it supports the Durkheimian idea behind this research that witch-hunting is not so much a function of demographic factors, such as population, but rather a function of the manner in which a collectivity is socially organized.

Our final control variable, government revenue, was positively related to the overall volume of deviance (beta = .36). As the communist nations constitute ten of the eleven one-party countries, assigning all of them the same value on the government revenue variable has created a problem of multicollinearity, making it difficult to determine the separate effects of the government revenue and party variables. Further evidence for the independent effect of state strength was found when internal security forces per thousand was used as the indicator and also had a statistically significant effect upon rates of witch-hunting (Bergesen, 1977:227).

This finding suggests that holding constant the effect of a nation's corporate organization—its party system, the relative strength of a nation's state seems to have an independent effect upon the overall volume of political deviance. There are at least two possible explanations for this finding.

Additional facilities for creating deviance. First, a stronger state suggests that it possesses an expanded governmental bureaucracy, state police, and larger military facilities, which would provide more institutional means for creating and labeling deviance. As we are coding ritualistic government activity, the stronger, and thereby we assume the larger or more expanded the web of governmental structure, the more institutional facilities there are for taking action. Similarly, the presence of an expanded governmental apparatus provides a series of positions, statuses, and organizations in which the "disease" of political subversion can be discovered. The mere increase in the apparatus of government, which we assume accompanies the increase in the relative strength of the state, would result in more agents of the collective purposes of the nation and hence in more institutional positions which could act to create political deviance.

Absence of opposition to purges and witch-hunts. The second line of reasoning derives from the early theorists of totalitarian societies. The stronger the state, the more freedom and power it possesses to conduct trials, investigations, or purges without being checked by other less powerful groups within the society. This does not say why a powerful state should have political deviance but, if it so decided, there would be less opposition than in more pluralistic societies where the diffusion of power over multiple groups prevents any one interest, particularly the government, from conducting a full-blown witch-hunt.

There are two possible research procedures which could be employed to help separate the effects of the corporate organization variable from the relative power of the state variable. The first would involve comparing a set of regimes which have a high degree of power concentration, but are not organized in terms of a political party, such as military regimes, with those states which are also powerful but have a party system, such as communist and African one-party countries. In this fashion, the power of the state would be held constant and the mode of corporate organization would be allowed to vary. If the theoretical model is correct, there should be less deviance in the strong states which do not possess a party system than in the ones with a party arrangement.

A second approach would be to develop a new coding scheme for just one-party states which would differentiate those which were more highly immanent. In the present research the comparison has been between one-party, two-party, and multi-party nations. What would be necessary would be to create a coding scheme whereby just one-party systems could be differentiated in terms of their organization as corporate entities and hence in terms of their degree of immanence. That is, although one-party systems are more highly immanent than either two-party or multi-party states, there is probably variation in the manner in which one-party states are organized, and hence in their relative degree of immanence.

Summary

In this chapter we examined the hypothesis that there was a direct relationship between the manner in which nations were organized as corporate entities and their rates of witch-hunting. The strongest effect was the party variable, with the control variables of economic development and ethno-linguistic heterogeneity showing negligible effects. A slightly larger positive effect was found with the population variable. The relative strength of the state also has a positive effect on the overall volume of political deviance, but was also highly correlated with the party variable. This finding was somewhat unexpected and two possible explanations were offered, along with a suggestion of research techniques for separating the effects of the corporate organization of a nation as opposed to the literal power of the state apparatus.

CHAPTER 5

CORPORATE ORGANIZATION AND THE DISTRIBUTION OF WITCH-HUNTING

In this chapter data relating to the hypothesis positing a relationship between the corporate organization of nations and the distribution of witch-hunting throughout their social structure will be examined. For every government action, such as accusations, arrests, trials, etc., the institutional areas in which individuals are accused of subversive activity were coded. The number of state activities defining deviance in any particular institutional area was the indicator of the relative distribution of witch-hunting throughout that nation's institutional space.

The Spread of Witch-Hunting Index

The spread of witch-hunting index is based on similar indexes which have been devised to measure population diversity.[29] For this analysis we have divided the institutional space of each nation into seven different, and mutually exclusive, institutional sectors: political, military, educational, professional, religious, industrial, and a category for references to foreigners. These areas are taken from the coding scheme (see Appendix II), and are composed of a number of more specific statuses within each general institutional area. These six areas, plus the category of foreigners, are as follows:

(1) *Political Institutions.*
- Executive leadership
- Representative bodies: congresses, legislatures, etc.
- The national bureaucracy
- Local or provincial government
(2) *Military Institutions*
- References to the military in general
- Top military officials
- Officer corp
- Enlisted men
(3) *Educational Institutions*
- Universities
- Colleges or technical schools
- Secondary schools
- Professors
- Students

---

[29]The specific formula used comes from Simpson (1949):

$$D = 1 - \sum_j \frac{N_i \, (N_i - 1)}{N(N-1)}$$

(4) *Professionals*
- Lawyers
- Newsmen
- Film industry
(5) *Religious Institutions*
- Reference to the church in general
- Church hierarchy (bishops, cardinals, etc.)
- Parish priests
- Reference to Catholics
- Reference to Jews
- Reference to sects: such as Jehovah's Witnesses
(6) *Industry*
- References to industry in general
- Management
- Labor Unions
- Workers
- Small businessmen
(7) *References to foreigners*
- Foreigners generally
- Agents of a foreign government: embassy personnel, diplomats, etc.

The index is based on the probability that any two randomly selected people labeled subversive by the witch-hunting activities of the state will appear in the same institutional sector. If the probability is high that they both come from the same institutional area, we can say that the distribution of witch-hunting across institutional areas is low. The higher the score on the spread of witch-hunting index the more the witch-hunt generated subversion is dispersed, or spread, throughout institutional space.

There is a bias in the computation of the Index for nations with small numbers of witch-hunting activities. Mexico, for instance, has three witch-hunting activities coded and each one is in a different institutional sector which gives Mexico a spread or dispersion score of 1.00. To help correct for this bias, those countries with less than 7 witch-hunting acts, which is the number of institutional categories we are using, are dropped from the sample for this analysis. This eliminates Mexico, Belgium, Norway, New Zealand, Ireland, and Iceland.

Once an Index score is computed for each nation, it is then entered as a piece of raw data into the regression equation which will include our independent variable, party system, and the other control variables. We are also including the overall number of deviants as a control variable to see if this dispersion of witch-hunting is affected by the overall rate of witch-hunting.

Findings

Table 5-1 presents the spread of witch-hunting index scores for each country in the sample, and the average Index score by type of party. One-party states have a mean spread score of .75, two-party states have a score of .72, and multi-party states a score of .63. The higher the score on the Index the more the discovered subversion is distributed across institutional categories. These scores indicate that as one moves from a multi-party to a one-party state, ritually created subversion is more dispersed throughout the social structure of these nations. Although the differences are not large, these findings clearly support the central hypothesis of this study.

Corporate Organization and the Spread of Witch-Hunting: A Multivariate Analysis.

This analysis is similar to that of Chapter 4. Our dependent variable, the spread of witch-hunting index is regressed against our independent variables of Party, Government Revenue, Percent Males in Agriculture, Ethno-linguistic Heterogeneity, Population, and Total Number of Deviants. The overall rate of witch-hunting was our dependent variable in Chapter 4, but here the concern is whether the overall volume of witch-hunting has any effect upon the relative dispersion of that witch-hunting throughout a nation's social structure.

Table 5-1
THE SPREAD OF WITCH-HUNTING INDEX SCORES*

Type of Corporate Organization

One-Party		Two-Party		Multi-Party	
Poland	.98	Australia	.76	Italy	.85
	(81)		(8)		(8)
Yugoslavia	.82	United States	.70	France	.77
	(79)		(189)		(40)
Hungary	.79	Great Britain	.69	Finland	.69
	(86)		(41)		(11)
Bulgaria	.76			Netherlands	.60
	(25)				(11)
Albania	.76			Denmark	.58
	(9)				(9)
U.S.S.R.	.75			Sweden	.55
	(63)				(9)
East Germany	.71			Switzerland	.39
	(101)				(9)
Czechoslovakia	.66				
	(160)				
Rumania	.65				
	(37)				
China	.58				
	(167)				
Mean = .75		Mean = .72		Mean = .63	
Std. Dev. = .11		Std. Dev. = .10		Std. Dev. = .14	
Median = .76		Median = .70		Median = .60	

*No Index score was computed for the following countries which had less than seven events: Mexico, New Zealand, Belgium, Norway, Ireland, Iceland.

After some preliminary analyses it became obvious that with the small number of cases the presence or absence of a few cases provided a source of instability within the data. For instance, with all of the nations of the sample in the analysis there is a negative relationship, with a beta of -.49, between a country's population and the dispersion of its witch-hunting. When, however, the Soviet Union and China are removed from the sample, the relationship changes to a + .46. Given this dramatic shift with the elimination of two cases it was decided to present the results of analysis in which (a) all the nations were entered, (b) China and the U.S.S.R. were eliminated, and finally (c) where the population variable was not entered into the regression equation. This analysis will be presented in a summary table facilitating comparisons between the three analyses and hopefully providing a more reliable understanding of the relationships between the variables.[30]

In Table 5-2 the independent variables we have been using throughout this research are again presented. They have been entered simultaneously into a regression equation along with the dependent variable, the spread of witch-hunting index. This is a summary table presenting only the beta coefficients. The matrix of zero-order correlations among these variables along with other statistical information pertinent to each of these runs can be found in Appendix II.

From this table we can see that the Party variable has consistent positive effects upon the dispersion of deviance even when controlling for the relative power of the state, level of economic development, social heterogeneity, population, and the total number of deviants. In conjunction with this finding, it is significant that no relationship was found between the relative power of the state and the distribution of witch-hunting. In the analysis of Chapter 4, the relative power of the state, as indicated by government revenue, had a positive effect upon overall rate of witch-hunting whereas in this analysis the relationship is non-existent. This is particularly significant given the high correlation between party and government revenue as mentioned in Chapter 4. This suggests that the rate of witch-hunting may not only be a function of the social organization of nations as corporate actors, but of the relative power of the state apparatus, whereas the relative distribution of witch-hunting seems to be only a function of the corporate organization variable.

These two findings support the central theoretical thrust of this research. Immanence, or the infusion of everyday istitutional life with ultimate values, is a function of the organization of a nation as a corporate actor and the ritual reaffirmation of that set of collective representations is performed by the creation of subversion. The more areas of social life infused with ultimate political meaning, the more areas in which political enemies are discovered.

Ethno-linguistic heterogeneity has a consistently small negative effect upon the spread of witch-hunting. This finding, along with the absence of an effect of heterogeneity upon the total number of witch-hunting acts, as found in Chapter 4, further supports the idea that the presence of diverse social groups within a nation does not result in a greater amount of political deviance. The idea that group conflict might be expressed in terms of charges of political subversion or treasonous activity is not supported here.

Economic development, as indicated by the percent males working in agriculture, shows consistently negative effects upon the spread of witch-hunting. This finding

---

[30]The removal of China and the Soviet Union, and the elimination of the population variable did not substantively effect the relationships between our independent variables and the dependent variable of Chapter 4, the overall number of witch-hunting activities.

Table 5-2
STANDARDIZED PARTIAL REGRESSION COEFFICENTS
FOR THE SPREAD OF WITCH-HUNTING INDEX AND INDEPENDENT VARIABLES

Independent Variables	Dependent Variable = Spread of Witch-Hunting Index		
	All Countries in the Analysis (N = 19)	All Countries except China and USSR (N = 17)	All Countries Population Variable Excluded (N = 19)
Political Party System	.26	.56	.41
Government Revenue, 1955	-.12	-.02	.03
Percent Males in Agriculture, 1955	.34	.14	.08
Ethno-linguistic Frationalization	-.26	-.29	-.19
Total Number of Witch-Hunting Acts	.33	-.05	-.02
Population, 1955	-.49	.46	--
Variance Explained (R^2)	.35	.55	.21

Note: Political Party System = Nation characterized by party system: one-party, two-party, multi-party.

Government Revenue = Government Revenue as a percent of total national income, from the World Tables (1971).

Percent Males in Agriculture = Percent of male workforce actively employed in agriculture, from ILO Project Series (1971).

Ethno-Linguistic Fractionlization = Degree of ethno-linguistic fractionalization from Atlas Narodov Mira (1971).

Witch-Hunting Activities = Total number of government events defining the presence of political deviance between 1950 and 1955.

Population = Country's population, from World Tables (1971).

Spread of Witch-Hunting Index = Population Diversity Index (Simpson, 1949).

reflects the presence of Eastern Europen countries, China, and the Soviet Union, all of which have both high spread scores and a higher percent of males in agriculture than the Western European States. The disporportionate effect of China and the Soviet Union is also seen when the negative relationship between males in agriculture and deviance dispersion drops when they are removed from the analysis.

The population and total number of witch-hunting activities variables are erratic and show dramatic changes with the removal of China and the Soviet Union. The substantive interpretation of these variables is difficult when the findings vary greatly with the removal of a few cases.

Summary

Although the number of cases in this analysis is small and the values of some of the variables changed dramatically with the removal of a few cases, the findings support the hypothesis of this research. The effect of the Durkheimian organization variable party system remains positive even when a series of control variables are entered into the analysis. The Swanson idea that more corporate collectivities should experience the sacred in the things and structures of daily life when combined with the Erikson notion that creating deviance (subversion) is a means for reaffirming collective sentiments helps explain the finding that more corporate states see more areas of their institutional infrastructure infected with all sorts of enemies and subversive elements.

CHAPTER 6
SUMMARY AND CONCLUSION

Political witch-hunts are a normal aspect of modern social life; they are not the unique creations of "totalitarian" systems. Although they take different forms, such as the Stalinist show trials or the McCarthy loyalty controversies, they perform the same social function of periodically renewing the collective representations of the modern state. Subversives, by definition, stand in opposition to all that the nation represents, and as such, their creation acts to dramatize the very meaning of national existence. Depending upon how a nation is structured as a corporate actor, ultimate national purposes can be immanent within the very definition of everyday life. The more highly immanent a nation, the more institutional areas there are infused with ultimate political significance, and hence more deviance will be created to ritually renew these collective political purposes.

These theoretical ideas generated the hypotheses that the greater the degree of immanence, the larger the volume of witch-hunting a nation will experience and the more dispersed it will be throughout that country's social space. To test these ideas, a coding scheme for detecting political deviance and for classifying nations in terms of their corporate organization was devised and data on 26 nations between 1950 and 1955 was gathered and analyzed.

The results support the two hypotheses. One-party states experienced more witch-hunting than two-party states, and they in turn experienced more than multi-party countries. This relationship was not eliminated with the introduction of control variables.

The second hypothesis, positing a link between corporate organization and the spread of witch-hunting was also supported. Witch-hunting was more extensively conducted in one-party than two-party states, and more in two party than multi-party states. As in the previous analysis, this relationship was not eliminated with the addition of control variables.

Although the most extreme instances of political terror and witch-hunting are associated with totalitarian regimes, the ritualistic search for imaginary enemies should be conceptualized as a variable, not the singular property of totalitarian states. The substance of the charges and accusations and the kinds of ritual may vary from country to country, but the sociological process is identical. Nations, as collectivities, are all searching for the same thing: the mythical enemy which stands in symbolic opposition to the nation as a corporate whole.

The reproduction of social reality through the complex interaction of ritual and a mythical universe populated with all sorts of extraordinary spirits and forces is similarly not the sole characteristic of primitive religious systems. The penetration of the sacred into daily reality is also a variable. Modern man also mingles and walks among his gods and finds himself in mortal combat with the mythical forces of Nature and History or The People and The Nation. These are Durkheimian representations of the corporate reality of modern societies, and the more corporate reality that is present, the stronger, more clearly defined and more closely merged with everyday reality are those symbolic representations. Daily life becomes filled with transcendent political significance and, simultaneously, the enemies of these sacred purposes. The ritual creation of oppositions to representations of corporate social reality is one of the fundamental forms of the modern religious life.

APPENDIX I

TABLE A-1
MATRIX OF ZERO-ORDER CORRELATIONS
(N = 25)

	Party	Gov Rev	Events	E-L Frac	Pop	Male Age
Party	1.00					
Gov Rev	.272*	1.00				
Events	.639	.521	1.00			
E-L Frac	.243	-.093	.200	1.00		
Pop	.235	.184	.408	.018	1.00	
Male Ag	.572	.123	.341	.004	.449	1.00

*When Mexico is removed from the sample, the correlation becomes .696.

Note: Party = Nation characterized by party system: one-party, two-party, multi-party.
   Gov Rev = Government revenue as a percent of total national income, from the World Tables (1971).
   Events = Total number of government events defining the presence of political deviance between 1950 and 1955.
   E-L Frac = Degree of ethno-linguistic fractionalization, from Atlas Narodov Mira (1971).
   Pop = Country's population, from World Tables (1971).
   Male Ag = Percent of male workforce actively employed in agriculture, from ILO Project Series (1971).

TABLE A-2
MATRIX OF ZERO-ORDER CORRELATIONS
(N = 19)

	Party	Gov Rev	Events	E-L Frac	Pop	Male Ag	Index
Party	1.00						
Gov Rev	.697	1.00					
Events	.722	.692	1.00				
E-L Frac	.229	-.013	.245	1.00			
Pop	.256	.228	.439	.008	1.00		
Male Ag	.547	.458	.361	.106	.463	1.00	
Index	.412	.336	.277	-.090	-.150	.288	1.00

Note: Party = Nation characterized by party system: one-party, two-party, multi-party.

Gov Rev = Government revenue as a percent of total national income, from the World Tables (1971).

Events = Total number of government events defining the presence of political deviance between 1950 and 1955.

E-L Frac = Degree of ethno-linguistic fractionalization, from Atlas Narodov Mira (1971).

Pop = Country's population, from World Tables (1971).

Male Ag = Percent of male workforce actively employed in agriculture, from ILO Project Series (1971).

Index = Measure of population diversity, taken from Simpson (1949).

TABLE A-3
MATRIX OF ZERO-ORDER CORRELATIONS
(N = 17)

	Party	Gov Rev	Events	E-L Frac	Pop	Male Ag	Index
Party	1.00						
Gov Rev	.670	1.00					
Events	.696	.671	1.00				
E-L Frac	.183	-.094	.261	1.00			
Pop	-.118	-.047	.247	-.028	1.00		
Male Ag	.517	.424	.222	.179	.184	1.00	
Index	.480	.389	.397	-.183	.416	.447	1.00

Note: Party = Nation characterized by party system: one-party, two-party, multi-party.

Gov Rev = Government revenue as a percent of total national income, from the World Tables (1971).

Events = Total number of government events defining the presence of political deviance between 1950 and 1955.

E-L Frac = Degree of ethno-linguistic fractionalization, from Atlas Narodov Mira (1971).

Pop = Country's population, from World Tables (1971).

Male Ag = Percent of male workforce actively employed in agriculture, from ILO Project Series (1971).

Index = Measure of population diversity, taken from Simpson (1949).

TABLE A-4
SPREAD OF WITCH-HUNTING INDEX
REGRESSED AGAINST INDEPENDENT VARIABLES*

Independent Variables	Dependent Variable: Spread of Witch-Hunting Index			
	B	Beta	Std. Error B	F
Political Party System	3.487	.26	5.558	.394
Government Revenue 1955	-.039	-.12	.172	.095
Percent Males in Agriculture, 1955	.002	.34	.002	1.088
Ethno-Linguistic Fractionalization	-.015	-.26	.015	1.043
Population, 1955	-.004	-.49	.002	2.612
Number of Witch-Hunting Activities	8.887	.33	11.646	.582
Variance Explained N = 19	(R^2):35			

*All Nations included in the analysis

Note: Political Party Systems = Nation characterized by party system: one-party, two-party, multi-party.

Government Revenue = Government Revenue as a percent of total national income, from the World Tables (1971).

Percent Males in Agriculture = Percent of male workforce actively employed in agriculture, from ILO Project Series (1971).

Ethno-Linguistic Fractionalization = Degree of ethno-linguistic fractionalization from Atlas Narodov Mira (1971).

Witch-Hunting Activities = Total number of government events defining the presence of political deviance between 1950 and 1955.

Population = Country's population, from World Tables (1971).

Spread of Witch-Hunting Index = Measure of population diversity, taken from Simpson (1949).

TABLE A-5
SPREAD OF WITCH-HUNTING INDEX
REGRESSED AGAINST INDEPENDENT VARIABLES*

Independent Variables	Dependent Variable: Spread of Witch-Hunting Index			
	B	Beta	Std. Error B	F
Political Party System	7.802	.56	5.971	1.707
Government Revenue 1955	-.006	-.02	.134	.003
Percent Males in Agriculture, 1955	.00099	.14	.002	.177
Ethno-Linguistic Fractionalization	-.018	-.29	.017	1.105
Population, 1955	.038	.46	.026	2.177
Number of Witch-Hunting Activities	-1.489	-.05	14.738	.010
Variance Explained N = 17	(R^2):.55			

*China and the U.S.S.R. excluded from the analysis.

Note: Political Party Systems = Nation characterized by party system: one-party, two-party, multi-party.
Government Revenue = Government Revenue as a percent of total national income, from the World Tables (1971).
Percent Males in Agriculture = Percent of male workforce actively employed in agriculture, from ILO Project Series (1971).
Ethno-Linguistic Fractionalization = Degree of ethno-linguistic fractionalization from Atlas Narodov Mira (1971).
Witch-Hunting Activities = Total number of government events defining the presence of political deviance between 1950 and 1955.
Population = Country's population, from World Tables (1971).
Spread of Witch-Hunting Index = Measure of population diversity, taken from Simpson (1949).

TABLE A-6
SPREAD OF WITCH-HUNTING INDEX
REGRESSED AGAINST INDEPENDENT VARIABLES*

Independent Variables	Dependent Variable: Spread of Witch-Hunting Index			
	B	Beta	Std. Error B	F
Political Party System	5.493	.41	5.744	.915
Government Revenue 1955	-.008	.03	.131	.004
Percent Males in Agriculture, 1955	.0005	.08	.0019	.074
Ethno-Linguistic Fractionalization	-.011	-.19	.015	.485
Number of Witch-Hunting Activities	-.444	.0165	10.723	.002
Variance Explained N = 19	(R^2):.21			

*Population variable deleted from the analysis

Note: Political Party Systems = Nation characterized by party system: one-party, two-party, multi-party.

Government Revenue = Government Revenue as a percent of total national income, from the World Tables (1971).

Percent Males in Agriculture = Percent of male workforce actively employed in agriculture, from ILO Project Series (1971).

Ethno-Linguistic Fractionalization = Degree of ethno-linguistic fractionalization from Atlas Narodov Mira (1971).

Witch-Hunting Activities = Total number of government events defining the presence of political deviance between 1950 and 1955.

Spread of Witch-Hunting Index = Measure of population diversity, taken from Simpson (1949).

APPENDIX II

Ritual Political Action Codes

Ritual Political Action—acts performed by a country's constituted political authorities in the definitional creation of political deviance.

Political Authorities—All collectiveties can be organized as corporate actors, possessing a structural arrangement for making collective decisions and taking collective action. In modern nation-states what we commonly refer to as a country's government represents that structural arrangement facilitating collective action by that society. In this study, political authorities are to include members of a country's government and members of a ruling party in one-party states. Members of military institutions, in that they also act as agencies of collective authortiy, are also to be included as political authorities. Ex-political office holders are to be excluded along with elites from other non-political institutions such as business or education elites. For example, a speech by a university president or ex-congressman on the presence of "communism" in schools would not be coded.

Political Deviance—nation-states also possess a set of distinctly corporate interests and purposes, commonly referred to as that country's national interest. Political crime is that activity defined by constituted political authorities as representing an attack upon, or a threat to, those national interests. What "actually" constitutes a threat to a country's national interest is irrelevant for this study. What is of concern is what that society defines as representing a threat to its interests, however they want to conceive those interests.

Coding Instructions

1. Ritual political acts and their characteristics are to be coded from the Index of the *New York Times* between the years 1950 and 1955.

2. Events are often mentioned more than once in the *Times* and are often listed under multiple headings. The Index should be read at least once to see if the same event is mentioned more than once, and on the second or third reading the event should be coded.

3. To cut down on exaggerated reports and misinformation all events that are reported from the press of another country should not be coded. When, for instance, the Italian press reports that some Yugoslav political figure is reportedly purged, arrested, or tried, these events will not be coded.

Columns	Code
Columns	*Code*
1-2	*Ritual political actions*—for every action taken by constituted political authorities in the identification or prosecution of political deviants, code one of the below categories.

01   *Warnings of dangers* and threats posed by the presence of subversive elements. Also code warnings that the nation is endangered by threats either from within or from other countries, and warnings that certain institutional practices could either increase deviance or endanger the nation.

02   *Specific charges* of subversives within organizations, institutions, or activities of individuals. Charge can be issued by an official, or a report, and can be done formally or in a speech or press conference.

03   *Discovery of plots*, conspiracies, spies, etc., within the country or within any particular institution. Include also reports of plots being squashed, thwarted, or aborted.

04   *Call for public action*, or vigilance to fight or thwart the expansion of deviance. These calls are to be made by government officials in the broad sense in which we use the term.

05   *Call for support of the nation*, state or its leaders, or call to reaffirm collective goals. Include urging of the reading of Chairman Mao, for instance.

06   *Proposed, pledged, or threatened actions* to thwart the growth of, spread of, or appearance of deviance. Include promised purges, requests for additional funds, or proposed laws to fight subversion.

07   *New laws, ordinances, executive decrees*, surveillance techniques, etc., to check the growth of political deviance.

08   *Restriction of activity*—restrictions on travel within the country, prohibiting groups from acting politically. Include barring priests from performing their roles.

09   *Expulsion of agents of foreign government*—include expulsion of embassy personnel, trade missions, or any other representatives.

10   *Deportations*, being asked to leave, expelled, etc., for either nationals or foreigners, but not for representatives of another government. Deportations *outside* of the country.

11   *Deportations*, etc., *within* the country.

12   *Arrests*, seizures, being held, etc.

58

Columns	Code

13   *Imprisonment*, jailed, tried, *sentenced*, or convicted of political crimes or activities related to political deviance.

14   *Resignations* where political influence in relationship to subversive activity is *clearly* indicated.

15   *Purges*—actual individuals being purged, or reference to purges being continued.

16   *Court actions*—new rulings in relationship to subversive activity, or to redefine the meaning of membership in the national political community.

17   Issue *supoenas, indictments*.

18   *Mass mobilizations*—rectification campaigns, indoctrination or re-education campaigns.

19   *Censorship campaigns*—banning of literature, art, cinema, etc., or constraints placed upon the press or other mass media, or changes in educational curricula to conform with political doctrines.

20   *Opening of major political trials*—where names of defendants or positions are mentioned.

21   *Sentences following major political trials*.

22   *Self-criticisms, confessions*, delivered in any context in relation to the commission of political crimes.

23   *Admission of deviant activity* or acknowledgement of deviant labels, such as admitting membership in the Communist Party during the HUAC hearings.

24   *Opening of government investigations*—code opening of new, or continuing investigations into subversive activity. Code all new HUAC hearings.

25   *Testifying* at government instigated investigation concerning subversive activity. The number of individuals testifying will be tabulated for three month periods. The total number of individuals testifying will then be coded. January will be the month code for the first quarter of the year, April for the second, July for the third, and October for the fourth quarter.

3-4   *Political authority instigating ritual action*—for every ritual political act code the relevant political authority taking that action. Where no authority is mentioned then code government generally. Code only agencies of the government, military or the system of federal courts. Do not code ex-political office holders or elites from other institutions.

01   Government generally, or mere reference to the ritual event.

02   Executive leadership—presidents, premiers, vice-premiers, etc.

03   Representative bodies—legislatures, congresses, parliaments, etc.

04   National bureaucracy—ministers, high government officials, federal agencies. Include the FBI or state police.

05   Government press or radio.

06   Party leaders (in one-party states).

07   Party press or radio.

08   Supreme court, or other national courts.

09   Lower federal courts—code reference to courts in general.

10   Federal grand jury.

11   Military—officials, press or radio.

5-6   *Characterization of ritual activity*—for every ritual act code the relevant type of deviant activity or political crime being defined.

01   Treason, spying, conspiracy.

02   Ideological typification—ultra-leftists, rightists, capitalist roaders, Titoites, Trotskyites, Slankyism, etc.

03   Terrorism, bombing assassination or charged with murder of government or party officials.

5-6   04   Inciting to riot, rioting, looting.

05   Sabotage, wrecking, suppressing revolutionary movements, misguiding the revolution, plotting.

06   Sacrificing the country or national interest to foreign interests, "selling out," etc.

Columns	Code	
	07	Personal interests threaten collective goals—profit motive, economism, bureaucraticism, problems of being red and expert, bourgeois thinking, etc.
	08.	Acting politically—attending meetings, reviving parties, etc.
	09	Attempting to flee the country.
	10	Constituting a security risk, or loyalty problem.
	11	Disrespect for national symbols—failure to salute, wear appropriate symbols, etc.
	12	Crimes of opinion—distribution of illegal or subversive literature, spreading rumors, possessing illegal literature, misusing religious feeling against the government.
	13	Subversive activity generally.
	14	Collaboration with known deviants, including aiding escapes.
	15	Failure to follow party line or government policy, or misusing government or party authority.
	16	Zionist.
	17	Communists, communist sympathizers.
	18	Fascists.
	99	Not mentioned, or not relevant.

7-8   *Institutional location of discovered deviancy*—for every ritual act which defines the presence of political deviants, code the institutional areas in which these subversive elements are discovered.

Columns	Code	
	01	Executive leadership—presidents, premiers, etc.
	02	Representative bodies—legislatures, parliaments, etc.
7-8	03	National bureaucracy—ministers, government agencies, etc.
	04	Local or provincial government—mayors, county officials, city government, etc.
	05	Party in general (all Party codes are only for one-party states).
	06	High Party officials—when titles are mentioned or reference to "top Party officials."
	07	Party leaders—when referred to as such.
	08	Party cadre—include local Party officials.
	09	Party youth organizations.
	10	Military—facilities, or references to the military generally, include references to army, air force, etc.
	11	Top military officials—chiefs of staff, heads of air force, etc.
	12	Officer corps.
	13	Enlisted men—rank and file military personnel.
	14	Universities.
	15	College or technical schools.
	16	Secondary schools.
	17	Professors or university administrators.
	18	Students, or youth generally
	19	Lawyers.
	20	Intellectuals—writers, artists, etc.
	21	Newsmen, newspapers, broadcasters, radio.
	22	Film industry, opera, ballet, theater.
	23	Reference to the Catholic Church in general.
	24	Church hierarchy—bishops, cardinals, etc.
	25	Parish priests.
7-8	26	Catholics—when not referred to as priests, bishops, etc.
	27	Jews.

Columns	Code	
	28	Sects—Jehovah's Witnesses, etc.
	29	Industry in general—factories, mills, plants, etc.
	30	Industrial management—factory managers, business executives, etc.
	31	Labor Unions.
	32	Workers.
	33	Small shops and businesses.
	34	Upper classes, Wealthy, Aristocracy, when referred to as such.
	35	Middle classes, bourgeoisie, etc., when referred to as such.
	36	Peasants, farmers, agricultural workers.
	37	Foreigners generally—businessmen, newsmen, students from other countries, etc.
	38	Agents of a foreign government—embassy personnel, etc.
	99	No institutional affiliation mentioned, or not relevant.
9-10		*Month* in which the event is reported.
	01	January
	02	February
	03	March
	04	April
	05	May
	06	June
	07	July
	08	August
	09	September
	10	October
	11	November
	12	December

11-12   *Punishment*—code the ritual event for each type of punishment. For instance if there are five sentenced to death, three sentenced for life, then code sentenced to death once, and sentenced to life once. Code the number sentenced under the "number of deviants" category.

Columns	Code	
11-12	01	Jailed or prison with no sentence mentioned.
	02	Jailed or prison: 0-2 years.
	03	Jailed or prison: 2-15 years.
	04	Jailed or prison: 15-life.
	05	Death—executions, hangings, etc.
	99	Not relevant, or not mentioned.

13-18   *Number of deviants reported*—the number of those tried, accused, arrested, and purged are often reported. Code the number mentioned, even though it may only be an estimate or an exaggerated report.

888 888   When the number mentioned is more than 888 888

999 999   When the number is not mentioned or not relevant.

Columns	Code	
19-21		*Country code*
	059	Mexico
	064	United States
	083	China
	116	Albania
	118	Belgium

Columns	Code	
	119	Bulgaria
	120	Czechoslovakia
	121	Denmark
	122	Finland
	123	France
	126	East Germany
	128	Hungary
19-21	129	Ireland
	130	Italy
	133	Netherlands
	134	Norway
	135	Poland
	137	Rumania
	139	Sweden
	140	Switzerland
	141	Great Britain
	144	Yugoslavia
	145	Australia
	148	New Zealand
	150	U.S.S.R.
	154	Iceland
22-23	*Year*—last two digits of the year in which the country is being coded.	

BIBLIOGRAPHY

Almond, Gabriel and G. Bingham Powell
1966   Comparative Politics: A Developmental Approach. Boston: Little, Brown.

Apter, David E.
1963   "Political Religion in the New Nations." In Clifford Geertz (ed.), Old Societies and New States. New York: The Free Press.

Arendt, Hannah
1973   The Origins of Totalitarianism. New Edition. New York: Harcourt, Brace, Jovanovich.

Atlas, Narodov Mira
1971   In Charles L. Taylor and Michael C. Hudson. Handbook of Political and Social Indicators. Vol. II. Ann Arbor: ICPR.

Banks, Arthur S. and Robert B. Textor
1963   A Cross-Polity Survey Cambridge: The MIT Press.

Banks, Arthur S.
1971   Cross-Polity Times Series Data. Cambridge: The MIT Press.

Baum, Richard and Louise B. Bennett (eds.)
1971   China in Ferment. Englewood Cliffs: Prentice-Hall.

Baum, Richard and Frederick C. Teiwes
1968   Ssu-ch'ing: The Socialist Education Movement 1962-1966. Berkeley: Center for Chinese Studies, University of California.

Bell, Daniel (ed.)
1964   The Radical Right. Garden City: Anchor.

Bellah, Robert N.
1967   "Civil Religion in America." Daedalus. 96 (Winter):1-21.

Bendix, Reinhard
1964   Nation-Building and Citizenship. New York: John Wiley.
1968   State and Society: A Reader in Comparative Political Sociology. Boston: Little, Brown and Co.

Bergesen, Albert
1977   "Political Witch-Hunts: The Sacred and the Subversive in Cross-National Perspective." American Sociological Review. 42 (April):220-233.
1978   "A Durkheimian Theory of Poltical Witch-Hunts with the Chinese Cultural Revolution of 1966-1969 as an Example." Journal for the Scientific Study of Religion. 17 (March):19-29.

Blondel, Jean
1968   "Party Systems and Patterns of Government in Western Democracies." Canadian Journal of Political Science 1:180-203.

Bridgham, Philip
1967   "Mao's 'Cultural Revolution': Origin and Development." The China Quarterly 29 (January-March):1-35.

Brzezinski, Zbigniew K.
1956   The Permanent Purge. Cambridge: Harvard University Press.

1958   "The Patterns of Political Purges." Pp. 79-87 in Henry L. Roberts (ed.), The Satellites in Eastern Europe. Vol. CCCXVII of The Annals of the American Academy of Political and Social Science.

Caute, David
1978   The Great Fear. New York: Simon and Schuster.

Coleman, James S., and Carl Roseberg, (eds.)
1964   Political Parties and National Integration in Tropical Africa. Berkeley: University of California Press.

Connor, Walter D.
1972   "The Manufacture of Deviance: The Case of the Soviet Purge, 1936-1938." American Sociological Review 37 (August):403-413.

Conquest, Robert
1968   The Great Terror. New York: Macmillan.

Currie, Elliott P.
1968   "Crime Without Criminals: Witchcraft and its Control in Renaissance Europe." Law and Society Review 3 (October):7-32.

Dallin, Alexander and George W. Breslauer
1970   Political Terror in Communist Systems. Stanford: Stanford University Press.

Douglas, Mary
1966   Purity and Danger. Harmondsworth: Penguin.
1970   Natural Symbols. New York: Pantheon.

Durkheim, Emile
1965   The Elementary Forms of the Religious Life. New York: The Free Press.
1933   The Division of Labor in Society. G. Simpson, translator. New York: MacMillan.

Eckstein, Harry
1962   Internal War: The Problem of Anticipation. A report submitted to the Research Group in Psychology and the Social Sciences, Smithsonian Institution, Washington, D.C.

Erikson, Kai T.
1966   Wayward Puritans: A Study in the Sociology of Deviance. New York: John Wiley.

Feierabend, Ivo K. and Rosalind Feierabend
1966   "Aggressive Behaviors Within Politics, 1948-62: A Cross National Study." Journal of Conflict Resolution 10:249-271.
1969   "Social Change and Political Violence: Cross National Patterns." Pp. 606-668 in H. D. Graham and T. R. Gurr (eds.), Violence in America: Historical and Comparative Perspectives. New York: New American Library.

Friedrich, Carl J., and Zbigniew K. Brzezinski
1956   Totalitarian Dictatorship and Autocracy. Cambridge: Harvard University Press.

Friedrich, Carl J., Michael Curtis and Benjamin R. Barber
1969   Totalitarianism in Perspective. New York: Praeger.

Goffman, Erving
1956   "The Nature of Deference and Demeanor." American Anthropologist 58 (June):473-502.

Goldman, Merle
1965   Literary Dissent in Communist China. Cambridge: Harvard University Press.

Goodin, Robert E.
1981   "Civil Religion and Political Witch-Hunts: Three Examples." Comparative Politics. 14 (October):1-15.

Gouldner, Alvin W.
1978   "Stalinism: A Study of Internal Colonialism." Telos. (Winter):5-48.

Greer, Donald
1935   The Incidence of the Terror During the French Revolution. Cambridge: Harvard University Press.

Gurr, Robert Ted
1968   "A Causal Model of Civil Strife: A Comparative Analysis Using New Indices." American Political Science Review 62 (December):1104-24.

Gusfield, Joseph R.
1963   Symbolic Crusade. Urbana: University of Illinois Press.

Hinton, William
1972   "Hundred Day War: The Cultural Revolution at Tsingua University." Monthly Review 24 (July-August):5-288.

Hodgkin, Thomas L.
1961   African Political Parties. Harmondsworth: Penguin Books.

Hofstader, Richard
1955   The Age of Reform. New York: Random House.

Huntington, Samuel P. and Clement H. Moore (eds.)
1970   Authoritarian Politics in Modern Society: The Dynamics of Established One-Party Systems. New York: Basic Books.

Inkeles, Alex
1968   Social Change in Soviet Russia. Cambridge: Harvard University Press.

International Labor Organization
1971   Labour Force Projections. Parts 1-5, I.L.O., Geneva.

Kilson, Martin L.
1963   "Authoritarian and Single-Party Tendencies in African Politics. World Politics 15 (January):262-294.

Kirchheimer, Otto
1966   "The Transformation of the Western European Party Systems." Pp. 177-200, in Jospeh LaPalombara and Myron Weiner (eds.). Political Parties and Political Development. Princeton: Princeton University Press.

LaPalombara, Joseph and Myron Weiner (eds.)
1966   Political Parties and Political Development. Princeton: Princeton University Press.

Lazarsfeld, Paul F. and Wagner Theilens, Jr.
1958   The Academic Mind. Glencoe: The Free Press.

Lee, Rensselaer W., III
1966   "The Hsia Fang System: Marxism and Modernisation." The China Quarterly 26 (April-June):68-81.

Lieberson, Stanley
1969   "Measuring Population Diversity." American Sociological Review 34 (December):850-862.

Lifton, Robert Jay
1968   Revolutionary Immortality. New York: Random House.

Lipset, S. M.
1955   "The Radical Right: A Problem for American Democracy." British Journal of Sociology 6 (June):176-209.
1960   "Party Systems and the Representation of Social Groups." European Journal of Sociology 1:50-85.
1963   The First New Nation. New York: Basic Books.

Lipset, S. M. and Stein Rokkan
1967   "Cleavage Structures, Party Systems, and Voter Alignments: An Introduction." Pp. 1-64 in Lipset and Rokkan (eds.), Party Systems and Voter Alignments. New York: The Free Press.

MacFarquhar, Roderick
1960   The Hundred Flowers Campaign and the Chinese Intellectuals. New York: Praeger.

Myrdal, Jan and Gun Kessle
1970   China: The Revolution Continued. New York: Random House.

Navasky, Victor
1980   Naming Names. New York: Viking Press.

Paige, Jeffrey M.
1971   Agrarian Social Movements and the Structure of Agricultural Export Sectors: A Cross-National Analysis. Proposal submitted to the National Science Foundation, Washington, D.C.

Palmer, Robert R.
1941   Twelve Who Ruled. Princeton: Princeton University Press.

Parsons, Talcott
1955   "Social Strains in America." Pp. 209-238 in Daniel Bell (ed.) The Radical Right. Garden City: Anchor.

Rae, Douglas W.
1967   The Political Consequences of Electoral Laws. New Haven: Yale University Press.

Rokkan, Stein
1966   "Electoral Mobilization, Party Competition, and National Integration." Pp. 224-265 in LaPalombara and Weiner (eds.), Political Parties and Political Development. Princeton: Princeton University Press.
1968   "Electoral Systems." Pp. 6-21 in David Sills (ed.), International Encyclopedia of the Social Sciences, Vol. 5 New York: Crowell-Collier-Macmillan.
1970   "Nation-Building, Cleavage Formation and the Structuring of Mass Politics." Pp. 72-144 in Stein Rokkan Citizens, Elections and Parties. New York: David McKay.

Rummel, Rudolph J.
1966   "Dimensions of Conflict Behavior Within Nations, 1946-59." Journal of Conflict Resolution 10 (March):65-74.

Russet et al.
1964   World Handbook of Political and Social Indicators. New Haven: Yale University Press.

Rustow, Dankwart, A.
1967   A World of Naitons. Washington, D.C.: The Brooks Institution.

Schacter, Ruth
1961   "Single Party Systems in West Africa." American Political Science Review 55 (June):294-307.

Schwartz, Benjamin
1968   "The Reign of Virtue: Some Broad Perspectives on Leader and Party in the Cultural Revolution." The China Quarterly 35 (July-Sept.):1-17.

Silver, Alan
1969   "Official Interpretations of Racial Riots" in Robert H. Connery (ed.), Urban Riots: Violence and Social Change. Proceedings of the Academy of Political Science 29 No. 1. New York.

Simpson, E. H.
1949   "Measurement of Diversity." Nature 163 (April 30):688.

Snyder, David and Charles Tilly
1972   "Hardship and Collective Violence in France, 1830 to 1960." American Sociological Review 37 (October):520-532.

Solomon, Richard H.
1971   Mao's Revolution and the Chinese Political Culture. Berkeley: University of California Press.

Sutton, Francis X
1959   "Representation and the Nature of Political Systems." Comparative Studies in Society and History 2:1-10.

Swanson, Guy E.
1964   The Birth of the Gods. Ann Arbor: University of Michigan Press.
1967   Religion and Regime. Ann Arbor: University of Michigan Press.

1971   "An Organizational Analysis of Collectivities." American Sociological Review 36 (August):607-623.

Tilly, Charles
1969   "Collective Violence in European Perspective." In H. D. Graham and T. Gurr (eds.), Violence in America: Historical and Comparative Perspectives. Washington, D.C.: National Commission on the Causes and Prevention of Violence.

Talmon, J. L.
19780   The Origins of Totalitarian Democracy. New York: W. W. Norton.

Tang Tsou
1969   "The Cultural Revolution and the Chinese Political System." The China Quarterly 38 (April-June):63-91.

Taylor, Charles L. and Michael C. Hudson
1971   Handbook of Political and Social Indicators. Vol. II. Ann Arbor: Inter-University Consortium for Political Research.

Tucker, Robert C.
1961   "Toward a Comparative Politics of Movement-Regimes." American Political Science Review 55 (1961):281-289.

Turner, Ralph
1969   "The Public Perception of Protest." American Sociological Review 34 (December):815-831.

Urban, George
1971   The Miracles of Chairman Mao. Los Angeles: Nash Publishing.

von der Mehden, Fred R.
1969   Politics of the Developing Nations. Englewood Cliffs: Prentice Hall.

Wallerstein, Immanuel
1961   Africa: The Politics of Independence. New York: Vintage Books.

Weber, Max
1948   The Theory of Economic and Social Organization. Glencoe: The Free Press.

World Tables
1971   International Bank for Reconstruction and Development. Economic Program Department, Socio-Economic Data Division.

INDEX